How to I Cryptocurrei ..oin, Defi and NFT - 2 Books in 1

Learn the Secrets to Build Generational Wealth During this Life Changing Bull Run

damages that may befall them after undertaking information described herein.

Additionally, the information in the following pages is intended only for informational purposes and should thus be thought of as universal. As befitting its nature, it is presented without assurance regarding its prolonged validity or interim quality. Trademarks that are mentioned are done without written consent and can in no way be considered an endorsement from the trademark holder.

Cryptocurrency for Beginners

A Comprehesive Guide to the World of Bitcoin, Blockchain and ERC-20 Tokens – Discover the Best Projects to Invest In During the Greatest Bull Run of All Time!

5

damages that may befall them after undertaking information described herein.

Additionally, the information in the following pages is intended only for informational purposes and should thus be thought of as universal. As befitting its nature, it is presented without assurance regarding its prolonged validity or interim quality. Trademarks that are mentioned are done without written consent and can in no way be considered an endorsement from the trademark holder.

Table of Contents

Introduction

Bitcoin has taken the world by storm once again when it crossed $20,000 per BTC in December of last year. After more than 2 years of bear market, the most famous cryptocurrency surpassed its previous all time high.

A lot of people are now trying to improvise themselves as professional investors and are losing a lot of money, only helping those who actually know what they are doing accumulate an incredible amount of wealth that will lead to generational fortunes.

To join the club of the few investors that actually make it, you need the right knowledge and the right mindset. Notice how we did not include a large initial capital. In fact, while having more money to invest means having more fire power, it is not necessary to have thousands of dollars to accumulate cryptocurrency and build wealth.

In fact, when we started investing in cryptocurrency we only had a few hundreds to put into the market, but that sum yielded us thousands and thousands of dollars over the span of a few years.

In this book you are going to discover everything there is to know about the fascinating world of cryptocurrency. From the operation of the Bitcoin blockchain to more advanced projects, like Uniswap and Compound.

If you diligently study the content of this book, we are sure you are going to see take your crypto knowledge to the next level. This also means you are going to see amazing results in a relative short period of time, since this bull run is offering an amazing number of opportunities.

To your success!

Kevin Anderson

Chapter 1 - An Introduction to ERC-20 Tokens

In previous chapters we have discussed how it is possible to create tokens on the Ethereum blockchain. Nowadays, most of the cryptocurrency there are in the world operate as ERC-20 tokens and do not have their own blockchain. This chapter dives deeper into this fascinating topic.

In the Ethereum ecosystem, ERC stands for Ethereum Request for Comment. These are technical documents that define the programming standards on Ethereum. They are not to be confused with the Ethereum Improvement Proposals (EIPs) which, like Bitcoin's BIPs, suggest improvements to the protocol itself. ERCs aim to establish conventions that make it easier for applications to interact with contracts.

Created in 2015 by Vitalik Buterin and Fabian Vogelsteller, ERC-20 proposes a relatively simple format for Ethereum-based tokens. By following these guidelines, developers don't need to reinvent the wheel every time they want to issue a token.

Instead, they can build on foundations already used throughout the industry.

Once created, the new ERC-20 tokens are automatically interoperable with services and software that support the ERC-20 standard (software wallet, hardware wallet, exchange, etc.).
It should be noted that the ERC-20 standard was developed in an EIP (specifically, EIP-20), a couple of years after the original proposal following its diffusion. However, even several years later, the name "ERC-20" remained.

Unlike ETH (Ethereum's native cryptocurrency), ERC-20 tokens are not held by accounts. Tokens exist only within a contract, structured similar to an independent database. The contract specifies the rules for the tokens (name, symbol, divisibility) and maintains a list that associates users' balances with their Ethereum addresses.

To move tokens, users must send a transaction to the contract asking to allocate part of their balance somewhere else. For example, if Alice wants to send 5,000 ExampleTokens to Bob, she broadcasts a request to a function within the ExampleTokens smart contract to do so.

Her request is contained in what appears to be a normal Ethereum transaction that pays 0 ETH to the token contract. The request is included in an additional field in the transaction, which specifies what Alice wants to do. In our case, she wants to transfer tokens to Bob.

Even if she is not sending ether, Alice still has to pay a fee in ETH to have her transaction included in a block. If she doesn't have any ETH, she has to buy some before transferring the tokens.

Now that we know the basics, let's take a deeper look to better understand the structure of a typical ERC-20 contract.

Creating ERC-20 tokens

To be compliant with the ERC-20 standard, your contract must include six mandatory functions: totalSupply, balanceOf, transfer, transferFrom, approve and allowance. Furthermore, you can specify optional functions, such as name, symbol and decimal. The purpose of these functions may be apparent from their names.

These are the functions as they appear in Solidity, the language created specifically for Ethereum.

totalSupply

function totalSupply () public view returns (uint256)

When called by a user, the function returns the total supply of tokens contained in the contract.

balanceOf

function balanceOf (address _owner) public view returns (uint256 balance)

Unlike totalSupply, balanceOf requires one parameter and that is the address. When called, it returns the token balance at that address. Remember that accounts on the Ethereum network are public, so you can analyze any user's balance if you know their address.

transfer

function transfer (address _to, uint256 _value) public returns (bool success)

Transfer sends tokens from one user to another. In this function, you have to enter the address to which you want to send the tokens and the amount to be transferred.

When called, transfer triggers what we call an event (in this case, a transfer event), which basically tells the blockchain to add a reference to it to the ledger.

transferFrom

function transferFrom (address _from, address _to, uint256 _value) public returns (bool success)

The transferFrom function is a useful alternative to transfer that offers a greater degree of programmability in decentralized applications. As a transfer, it is used to move tokens, but these tokens do not necessarily have to belong to the person making a request to the contract.

In other words, you can authorize someone to transfer funds on your behalf. A possible use case involves paying for service subscriptions, where you don't want to manually send a payment every day / week / month. Instead, you just let a program do it for you.

This function triggers the same transfer event over and over.

approves

function approve (address _spender, uint256 _value) public returns (bool success)

Approve is another useful programmability feature. With this feature, you can limit the number of tokens a smart contract can withdraw from your balance. Without it, you run the risk that a contract malfunction will lead to zeroing of all your funds.

Let's take the example of a subscription model again. Suppose you have a large amount of ExampleTokens, and you want to set up recurring weekly payments to a DApp that offers streaming services. You're busy reading this book day and night, so you don't want to waste time each week manually creating a transaction.

You have a large ExampleTokens balance, far more than you need to pay for the subscription. To prevent the DApp from draining all your funds, you can set a limit with the "approve" function. Let's assume your subscription costs 1 ExampleTokens per week. If you limit the approved value to five tokens, your subscription will be paid automatically for five months.

At worst, if the DApp tries to withdraw all your funds you can only lose twenty tokens. It might not be an ideal scenario, but it's definitely better than losing every ExampleToken you own.

When called, approve triggers the approval event. Like the transfer event, it adds data to the blockchain.

allowance

function allowance (address _owner, address _spender) public view returns (uint256 remaining)

Allowance can be used in conjunction with the "approve" function. When you give the contract permission to manage your tokens, you could use this feature to check how many tokens it can still withdraw. For example, if your subscription used three of the five approved tokens, the allowance function should return a total of two.

Optional functions

The functions outlined above are mandatory. Instead, name, symbol and decimal don't have to be included, but they can enhance your ERC-20 contract. Respectively, they allow you to add a name in a readable form, set a ticker (e.g., ETH, BTC, BNB) and specify how many decimal places the token can be divided into. For example, tokens used as currencies could benefit more from divisibility than tokens representing property ownership.

The power of ERC-20 tokens

By combining all the functions we have talked about, we can build an ERC-20 contract. We can request full supply, check balances, transfer funds and give permissions to other DApps to manage tokens on our behalf.

One of the characteristics that explain the attractiveness of ERC-20 tokens is their flexibility. Established conventions do not limit development, so developers can implement additional functionality and set specific parameters to meet their needs.

Stablecoins

Stablecoins (tokens pegged to fiat currencies) often use the ERC-20 standard. The BUSD transaction we mentioned earlier is just an example, and most of the major stablecoins are also available in this format.

For a typical fiat-backed stablecoin, the issuer holds reserves in euros, dollars, etc. Then, for each unit in the reserve, it issues a token. This means that if $10,000 is locked in the safe, the issuer can create 10,000 tokens, each redeemable for $1.

On a technical level, this is pretty simple to set up on Ethereum. The issuer simply has to launch a contract with 10,000 tokens. Later, it will distribute them to users with the promise of being able to redeem them in the future for a certain sum of fiat money.

Users can use these tokens for a variety of purposes. For instance, they can buy goods and services or use them in DApps. Alternatively, they can request the issuer to exchange them for fiat. In this case, the issuer burns the returned tokens and sends the corresponding amount of fiat from the reserve.

The contract governing this system, as already mentioned, is relatively simplistic. However, launching a stablecoin requires a lot of work on external factors such as logistics and regulatory compliance.

Security token

Security tokens are similar to stablecoins. At the contract level, both could even be identical as they work the same way. The distinction occurs at the issuer level. Security tokens represent financial instruments, such as stocks, bonds or physical assets. Oftentimes, they guarantee the holder some form of participation in an asset or commodity.

Utility token

Utility tokens are perhaps the most common type of token today. Unlike the previous two, they are not backed by anything. While asset-backed tokens can be compared to airline stock, utility tokens are similar to frequent-flyer programs. They have a function, but they have no external value. Utility tokens can satisfy a myriad of use cases, acting as in-game currency, fuel for decentralized applications, loyalty points, and more.

Is it possible to mine ERC-20 tokens?

You can mine ether, but ERC-20 tokens are not mineable. We use the term coined when new ones are created. When a contract is launched, developers distribute the supply according to their plans and roadmap.

Typically, this is done through Initial Coin Offering (ICO), Initial Exchange Offering (IEO) or Security Token Offering (STO). You may come across variations of these acronyms, but the concepts are quite similar to each other. Investors send ether to the contract address and, in return, receive new tokens. The funds raised are used to finance the further development of the project. Users expect to be able to use their tokens or to be able to resell them at a higher price during the development of the project.

Token distribution doesn't have to be automated. Many crowdfunding events allow users to pay with a variety of digital currencies (such as BNB, BTC, ETH and USDT). The respective balances will then be allocated to the addresses indicated by the users.

Pros of ERC-20 tokens

Fungible

ERC-20 tokens are fungible. each unit is interchangeable with another. If you own an ExampleToken, it doesn't matter what the specific token is. You can exchange it for someone else's, and they will still be functionally identical, like cash or gold.

This property is ideal if the token aims to perform the function of a coin. For this use case the individual units cannot have distinctive traits, as they would be non-fungible. This could lead to some tokens being more valuable than others, compromising their purpose.

Flexible

As we saw in the previous section, ERC-20 tokens are highly customizable and can be used in many different applications. For example, we can use them as in-game currency, in loyalty programs, as digital collectibles, or even to represent works of art and property rights.

Popular

The popularity of ERC-20s in the cryptocurrency industry is a very compelling reason to use this standard as a model. There are a myriad of exchanges, wallets and smart contracts already compatible with the newly launched tokens. Plus, developer support and documentation are plentiful.

Cons of ERC-20 tokens

Scalability

As with many other cryptocurrency networks, Ethereum is not immune to scaling issues. In its current form, it is not scalable. In fact, trying to send a transaction during peak hours results in high costs and delays. If you throw an ERC-20 token and the network becomes congested, its usability may be affected.

It is not a problem exclusive to Ethereum, but a necessary compromise for security in distributed systems. The community intends to address these issues in the migration to Ethereum 2.0, which will implement updates such as Ethereum Plasma and Ethereum Casper.

Scams

While it's not a problem with the technology itself, the ease with which tokens can be created can be seen as a downside in some ways. It takes minimal effort to create a simple ERC-20 token, so anyone can do it.

Consequently, you should be very careful what you invest in. There are several pyramid and Ponzi schemes disguised as blockchain projects. Do the necessary research before investing and decide for yourself whether an opportunity is legitimate or not.

ERC-20, ERC-1155, ERC-223, and ERC-721

ERC-20 was the first standard for Ethereum tokens, but it is by no means the only one. Over the years, many others have emerged, proposing improvements to ERC-20 or trying to achieve entirely different goals.

Some of the less common standards are those used for non-fungible tokens. Sometimes, some use cases require tokens that are unique and have different attributes. If you want to tokenize a unique work of art, or an in-game asset, one of these contracts might be more appropriate.

The ERC-721 standard, for example, was used for the very popular DApp CryptoKitties. Such a contract presents users with an API to mint their own non-fungible tokens and encode metadata.

The ERC-1155 standard can be considered an improvement of ERC-721 and ERC-20. It defines a standard that supports both fungible and non-fungible tokens in the same contract.

Other options like ERC-223 or ERC-621 aim to improve usability. The first implements security measures to prevent accidental token transfers. The second adds extra features to increase and decrease the token supply.

The ERC-20 standard has dominated the crypto asset industry for years, and it's not hard to see why. With relative ease, anyone can implement a simple contract that satisfies a wide range of use cases. That said, ERC-20 lacks some of the functionality introduced by other standards. It remains to be seen whether any of the subsequent contract types will take its place.

In the next chapters we are going to take a look at some of the most interesting ERC-20 tokens there are today. We have invested in all these tokens and we highly recommend you study them very carefully.

Chapter 2 - ChainLink (LINK)

Chainlink has become one of the most used projects in the cryptocurrency industry. It is a service that offers decentralized oracles that can provide external data to smart contracts on Ethereum. In other words, it connects blockchains with the real world.

You can imagine Chainlink as a committee of wise men always striving to determine the closest thing to the truth.

Smart contracts automate agreements on the blockchain. They evaluate the available information and, when certain conditions are met, they are executed. However, this presents a problem. Blockchains don't have a reliable way to access external data. The difficulty of linking off-chain data with on-chain data is one of the great challenges of smart contracts.

Chainlink tries to solve this problem by providing a decentralized oracle service. In short, an oracle is a program that translates external data into a language understandable for smart contracts, and vice versa.

What is Chainlink?

Chainlink is a blockchain-based decentralized oracle network that allows smart contracts to connect to external data sources. These can include APIs, internal systems, or other types of feeds. LINK is an ERC-20 token used to pay for this oracle service on the network.

A decentralized oracle

First of all, we need to understand what a centralized oracle is. It's not that hard to guess - it's a single information provider outside a smart contract. It's just a source. This can present significant problems. What happens if an oracle provides false or incorrect data? All systems that depend on it will fail. This scenario is often referred to as "the oracle problem". That is what Chainlink tries to solve.

How Chainlink works

Chainlink uses a network of nodes in an attempt to make the data provided to smart contracts as reliable and trustworthy as possible.

Suppose a smart contract requests data from the real world, and that it communicates a request for that purpose. The Chainlink protocol records this event and transmits it to the Chainlink nodes to collect their "offers" on the request.

What makes this process important is how Chainlink can validate data from multiple sources. Thanks to an internal reputation system, Chainlink can determine with relatively high accuracy which sources should be trusted. This can greatly increase the accuracy of results and protect smart contracts from all sorts of attacks.

So how does all this relate to LINK? Well, smart contracts requesting data pay Chainlink node operators with LINK in exchange for their services. Prices are set by node operators based on market conditions for such data.

Additionally, node operators stake the network to ensure long-term commitment to the project. Similar to Bitcoin's crypto economic model, Chainlink's node operators are incentivized to act reliably instead of harming the system.

Chainlink and DeFi

Since decentralized finance has become more popular, high-quality oracle services have sparked increasing interest. After all, most of these projects use smart contracts in one way or another, and require external data to operate properly.

With centralized oracle services, DeFi platforms can be vulnerable to a wide range of attacks, including flash loan attacks through oracle manipulation. Several incidents have already occurred, and will likely continue to occur accompanying the use of centralized oracles.

Many people may be inclined to think that Chainlink is capable of solving all of these problems. However, this may not be accurate. In fact, while projects like Synthetix, Aave and others rely on Chainlink's technology, new types of risk are being introduced. If too many platforms depend on the same oracle service, they will fail in case Chainlink suddenly stops working as it should.

This scenario might seem unlikely. After all, Chainlink is a decentralized oracle service that supposedly doesn't have a single point of failure. However, in September 2020, the Chainlink nodes suffered a "spam attack" in which the hacker potentially stole up to 700 ETH from the operators' wallets. The attack was resolved, but it reminds us that not all systems are fully resilient to malicious activity, even if they are decentralized.

The offer and issue of LINK

LINK has a maximum supply of 1 billion tokens. 35% of these were sold during an ICO in 2017. About 300 million are in the hands of the company that founded the project.

Unlike many other crypto assets, LINK does not have a mining or staking process that increases the supply in circulation.

How to store LINK

LINK does not have a native blockchain. It exists as a token on the Ethereum blockchain. LINK tokens follow the ERC-667 standard, an extension of the ERC-20 standard. In short, you can store LINK in any supported wallet, such as Trust Wallet or MetaMask.

Use cases for LINK

As we mentioned, node operators can stake LINK to present an offer to the potential data buyer. The operator who "wins" must provide the information to the smart contract that sent the request. All payments to node operators are in the form of LINK tokens.

This approach encourages node operators to continue accumulating the tokens. Why? Because owning more tokens means being able to access ever larger data contracts. If an operator decides to break the rules, they will be punished with the removal of their LINK tokens.

LINK Marines

It is not uncommon for crypto projects to give their community members a nickname. Chainlink was one of the most obvious early examples with its "LINK Marines."

This type of community creation is becoming an increasingly effective marketing tactic in the cryptocurrency industry. Nicknames can create a lot of social media engagement and attention for the project.

Chainlink's technology has proven to be one of the main pillars of DeFi and the crypto ecosystem as a whole. While it introduces risks into DeFi on Ethereum, reliable external data sources are one of the most important building blocks for a robust ecosystem of on-chain products.

We purchased LINK at around $5 per token back in June 2020. We are still holding them.

Chapter 3 - Aave (AAVE)

AAVE is the native governance token of the Aave protocol. Holders of the Ethereum-based cryptocurrency can discuss and vote on proposals that influence the direction of the project.

As Aave is one of the leading decentralized finance protocols, the AAVE token is one of the largest DeFi coins by market cap. Ethereum investors can borrow and lend their cryptocurrencies in a decentralized way through Aave.

The foundation of any financial ecosystem is the means by which individuals can borrow and lend their assets. Borrowing allows you to take advantage of capital to carry out activities, while granting loans allows you to earn a regular and safe return thanks to your capital.

Cryptocurrency developers have recognized the need for such services by launching so-called money markets. Aave is one of the largest and most successful of these platforms.

What Aave is

Aave is an Ethereum-based money market where users can lend and borrow across a wide range of digital assets, from stablecoins to altcoins. The Aave protocol is governed by AAVE owners.

It will be difficult to understand what the AAVE token is without understanding the underlying Aave protocol, so let's start from there.

ETHLend

Aave's origins date back to 2017. Stani Kulechov and a team of developers launched ETHLend in an Initial Coin Offering (ICO) in November 2017. The idea was to allow users to lend and borrow cryptocurrencies to each other by allowing them to publish loan requests and offers.

Even though ETHLend was an innovative idea, the platform, along with its LEND token, lost momentum during the bear market in 2018. The main weaknesses of the platform were the lack of liquidity and the difficulty in matching requests and loan offers.

Then, during the bear market of 2018 and 2019, the ETHLend team rebranded their product, releasing Aave in early 2020.

In a podcast, Kulechov explained that the bear market was one of the best things that could happen to ETHLend. This period provided the team with the opportunity to revamp the concept of decentralized crypto lending, creating what we know today as Aave.

How Aave works

The concept of the new Aave is similar to that of ETHLend. Both allow Ethereum users to borrow cryptocurrency or make money by lending their own funds. However, they are profoundly different from a technical point of view.

Aave is an algorithmic money market, so loans are obtained from a pool instead of being individually matched to a lender.

The interest rate charged depends on the "utilization rate" of the assets in a pool. If almost all the assets in a pool are used, the interest rate will be high to persuade liquidity providers to deposit more capital. If few assets are used in a pool, the interest rate charged is low to incentivize loans.

Additionally, Aave allows users to take out loans in a different cryptocurrency than the one they deposited. For example, a user can deposit Ethereum and withdraw stablecoins to be deposited into Yearn.finance to earn a regular return.

Like ETHLend, all loans are extra-collateralized. This means that if a user wants to take out a $100 cryptocurrency loan through Aave, they must deposit more than this amount.

Due to the volatility of cryptocurrencies, Aave integrates a liquidation process. If the collateral you provide falls below the collateralization ratio specified by the protocol, your collateral may be liquidated. Furthermore, a commission is applied in the event of liquidation. Make sure you understand the risks associated with depositing funds into Aave before allocating collateral.

Other key functions

Aave is expanding its reach far beyond the money markets. The platform has gained popularity as a place where DeFi users can get flash loans.

Often, Aave's money market pools have much more liquidity than borrowers' loans. This unused liquidity can be used for flash loans, which are collateral-free loans that exist only within an Ethereum block.

Basically, a flash loan allows a user to borrow a large amount of cryptocurrency without allocating collateral, and repay the loan within the same transaction (as long as they pay the one-block interest fee).

This allows those with large amounts of capital to arbitrage and take advantage of other opportunities, all in a single blockchain transaction. For example, if you see that Ether is priced at 500 USDC on Uniswap and 505 USDC on another decentralized exchange, you can try to take advantage of the price difference by borrowing a large sum of USDC and making quick trades.

In addition to flash loans and other features, Aave is also working on a non-fungible token-based (NFT) video game called Aavegotchi.

The AAVE token

When ETHLend became Aave, the LEND token remained active. This was a problem, as LEND didn't have the code to work the way the team wanted. Specifically, LEND owners could not control the direction of the Aave protocol.

This problem became more and more relevant as Aave attracted more and more liquidity and its users could not promote protocol changes. Hence, a transition of LEND to a new currency called AAVE was proposed, with a ratio of 100 LEND to 1 AAVE.

AAVE, as a new Ethereum-based ERC-20 token, has brought with it a number of new use cases.

First of all, AAVE owners act as a safety net for the protocol. The release of AAVE introduces a new concept called the "Safety Module," which protects the system from a capital shortage. This means that if there is not enough capital in the protocol to cover creditors' funds, the AAVE tokens in the Safety Module will be sold for the assets needed to cover the deficit.

Only the AAVEs deposited in the form will be cleared for the deficit. Deposits in the module are incentivized with a regular return paid in AAVE.

The second main use case of AAVE is related to the governance of the Aave protocol. Holders of the cryptocurrency can discuss and vote on Aave Improvement Proposal, which can be implemented if accepted by a minimum number of AAVE tokens. These proposals may include changes to Aave's money market parameters, as well as managing funds in the ecosystem reserve. As with many other governance tokens, one AAVE corresponds to one vote.

AAVE further decentralizes the DeFi application and adds important ecosystem support to mitigate black swan events.

The challenges for Aave

A challenge faced by Aave is the fact that all loans are extra-collateralized. Unlike the traditional financial system, there is no credit score system or procedure that allows you to systematically determine whether or not the borrower will be able to repay the loan.

This means that, unlike traditional loans offered by banks, which may require minimal formal collateralisation, Aave users must block cryptocurrencies worth more than the requested loan.

This limitation implies that Aave is a capital inefficient system. Aave requires users to commit large amounts of capital to obtain loans, making it difficult for small users to use the protocol. While this measure is intended to protect creditors, the system naturally limits the size of Aave's aggregate debt.

Decentralized money markets such as Aave pave the way for a more open and accessible financial system. Aave is an interesting DeFi project that allows crypto users to access funds and services transparently.

The AAVE token is also a promising development. It allows its owners to influence changes in the Aave protocol. It also protects the protocol from black swan events.

We have invested in AAVE back when the token was called LEND and we are still holding our funds.

Chapter 4 - MakerDAO and DAI

Stablecoins have emerged as a kind of middle ground between the traditional financial market and the nascent universe of digital assets. Following the value of a fiat currency and operating as cryptocurrencies, these blockchain-based tokens were initially appealing to traders as a way to "lock in" their profits.

To date, the most popular type of stablecoin is the one guaranteed by fiat. Typically, these tokens are backed by USD. Therefore, they hold their value because there is a bank account with an equivalent dollar amount. In other words, each token is worth $1 and it should be possible to exchange it for cash at any time. Some of the most popular stablecoins are USDT, USDC, BUSD, and PAX.

In this chapter, we'll take a look at a protocol called Maker, or MakerDAO. This innovative stablecoin system focuses on what we call crypto collateralisation. Basically, it eliminates the need for the bank account we just described.

What MakerDAO is

Maker is an Ethereum-based system that allows users to issue DAI, a token that replicates the price of the US dollar. No single entity is in command. Instead, the participants hold the governance token (MKR), which gives them voting rights on changes to be made to the protocol. It is from this aspect that the DAO (Decentralized Autonomous Organization) component of the name derives. In fact, the protocol is effectively governed by a distributed network of stakeholders who own MKR tokens.

In this decentralized ecosystem, smart contracts and game theory allow DAI to maintain a relatively stable value. Aside from that, it is functionally identical to fiat-backed counterparties. You can send it to friends and family, use it to buy goods and services, or stake it in yield farming.

DAI is "backed by crypto"

When you provide collateral, you block something of value in exchange for a loan. When you repay the loan, you will get this something back. Imagine a pawnshop, where you can hand over your jewelry in exchange for cash. After that, you have a certain period to buy back the jewel by returning the funds.

If you don't return the money, the pawnshop can simply sell your jewelry to recoup the losses. In this way, the collateral offers a guarantee. The same principle is also applied by banks. For example, you can offer a car or a house as collateral in exchange for a loan.

Similarly, a fiat-backed stablecoin is collateralized by fiat money. A user delivers cash and receives tokens in exchange. Afterward, they can return the tokens to the issuer, but if they don't, the issuer keeps the cash.

A crypto-backed stablecoin such as DAI works in a similar way, but you can use crypto assets as collateral. Furthermore, the issuer is simply a smart contract. Basically, the contract says something like: you issue X amount of tokens for every Y amount of ETH deposited. Return a Z amount of ETH when the tokens are returned.

Over-collateralisation and CDPs

You've probably noticed that crypto markets are quite volatile. We often see the price of BTC, ETH and other cryptocurrencies changing rapidly. Your assets could be worth $4,000 when you go to sleep and $3,000 when you wake up. For a lender, this is very risky. Take gold jewelry as an example, they can expect it to remain relatively stable in value. If you don't repay your loan, the lender can simply sell the jewelry to get the money back.

If you get a $400 loan (blocking 1 ETH equal to $400 as collateral) and the price of ETH drops to $300, the lender will lose. It may ask you to block more ETH as collateral or liquidate it and lose $100.

This is why Maker uses the concept of over-collateralisation. It's a difficult word, but the idea is simple. When a debtor wants to issue DAI stablecoins, they provide more collateral than the amount they want to borrow. This way, even if the price falls, the position will still be hedged.

In practice, users lock their ether (or other supported assets) in so-called collateralized debt positions (CDP). At the time of writing, they must provide collateral equal to at least 150% of the value of the DAI they are borrowing. In other words, if you want to issue 400 DAI (remember, each token is worth $1), you'll need to provide collateral equal to $600 in ETH.

A user can add more collateral if they wish to do so. In fact, most do it for safety. However, if the amount of collateral falls below 150%, they will face a heavy penalty. Eventually, the user risks liquidation if they do not repay the DAI with interest. The interest is also called Stability Fee.

Keeping a stable value

As we said, 1 DAI = 1 USD (more or less). But why?

Well, it's all about incentives and smart contracts. When DAI falls below the target price, the system makes closing CDPs through debt repayment more attractive to users. It raises interest rates to do so. This reduces the total supply of DAI, as the repaid funds are destroyed. If the price exceeds one dollar, the opposite happens. In this case, users are incentivized to open CDPs by reducing interest rates. This creates new DAI and increases the total supply.

The use cases for DAI

As already mentioned, you can use DAI like any other stablecoin. You exchange it for other cryptocurrencies, use it to buy goods and services, or even destroy it for fun. If you don't want to deal with CDP or other complicated processes, no problem. Similar to other cryptocurrencies, you can buy DAI on exchanges like Binance.

MakerDAO was probably one of the first decentralized finance protocols. After all, DAI is a decentralized stablecoin and DeFi aims to create a "financial system on the blockchain." It doesn't get more DeFi than this.

The list of products and services that accept DAI continues to grow. You may have noticed some decentralized applications where you can use it. Among these we find PoolTogether and SushiSwap, in addition to the myriad of systems for yield farming.

As the main crypto-backed stablecoin, DAI proved to be a successful experiment in creating a token that accurately tracks the price of the US dollar. The protocol mitigates the volatility present in traditional digital currencies, moving away from the traditional financial world towards a native digital ecosystem.

We have invested in the project in 2020 and we have no plan to sell our tokens any time soon.

Chapter 5 - The Compound Protocol

Compound Finance is a tool that allows you to lend or borrow cryptocurrencies. All you need is an Ethereum wallet, some funds, and you can get loans or receive interest immediately. Providing assets to Compound is very simple, and your funds are never in the hands of a third party.

The user experience is quite fluid, and the protocol has been tested in the real world for some time. Additionally, many yield farmers use Compound to borrow assets and supply them to other DeFi protocols.

What is Compound Finance?

Compound Finance is a DeFi loan protocol. In more technical terms, it is an algorithmic money market. You could imagine it as an open market for several coins. It allows users to deposit cryptocurrencies and earn interest, or borrow other crypto assets as collateral. Use smart contracts that automate the storage and management of capital added to the platform.

Any user can connect to Compound and earn interest using a Web 3.0 wallet such as Metamask. For this reason Compound is a permissionless protocol, anyone with a crypto wallet and an internet connection can interact with it freely.

On Compound, lenders and borrowers don't have to negotiate terms as they would in a more traditional setting. Both parties interact directly with the protocol, which manages collateral and interest rates. No counterparty holds the funds, as the assets are held in smart contracts called liquidity pools.

The interest rates for granting and borrowing on Compound are adjusted algorithmically. This means that the Compound protocol automatically adjusts them based on supply and demand. Additionally, COMP token holders also have the power to make changes to interest rates.

How Compound Finance works

Assets supplied in Compound are tracked using cToken, Compound's native tokens. CTokens are ERC-20 tokens that represent shares of an asset pool in Compound.

For example, if you deposit ETH on Compound, it is converted to cETH. If you deposit the DAI stablecoin, it is converted to cDAI. If you deposit multiple coins, each will accumulate interest based on individual rates. In other words, cDAI will earn cDAI's interest rate and cETH will earn cETH's interest rate.

CTokens can be redeemed for the portion of the pool they represent, making the provided assets available in the linked wallet. As the money market accumulates interest, cTokens become convertible with a larger portion of the underlying asset. In essence, this means that to earn interest on Compound you simply need to keep an ERC-20 token.

The process begins with the user connecting a Web 3.0 wallet, such as Metamask to the protocol. Afterward, they can select any unlockable assets they want to interact with. If an asset is unlocked, users can check it out or borrow it.

Granting loans is very simple. Unlock the asset you want to provide as cash, and sign a transaction through your wallet to start providing capital. Assets are instantly added to the pool, and start earning interest in real time. Through this step the assets are converted into cToken.

Borrowing, on the other hand, is a bit more complicated. First of all, users deposit funds as collateral for the loan. In return, they get the "Borrowing Power," needed to borrow on Compound. Each asset available for supply will add a different amount of Borrowing Power. At this point, users can borrow based on how much Borrowing Power they have available.

Like MakerDAO, Compound works on the concept of overcollateralization. This means that borrowers must provide more value than they wish to borrow to avoid liquidation.

It should be emphasized that each asset has a unique Annual Percentage Rate (APR) for loan and supply. Since rates are adjusted on the basis of supply and demand, each asset will have a unique interest rate for both granting and borrowing. As we have already mentioned, each asset will earn at different interest rates.

Assets supported by Compound Finance
As of 22/04/2020, the assets supported for borrowing and disbursing loans on Compound are the following:

- ETH

- WBTC (Wrapped Bitcoin)

- USDC

- COME ON

- USDT

- ZRX

- BAT

- REP

Additional tokens will likely be added in the future.

Compound's governance

Compound was launched as a venture capital-funded company founded by Robert Leshner. However, Compound Finance governance is gradually becoming more decentralized thanks to the COMP token. The token grants holders a share of the fees and governance rights on the protocol.

Therefore, COMP holders can make changes to the protocol through improvement proposals and on-chain voting. Each token represents one vote, and holders can vote on proposals using their own balance sheets. In the future, the protocol may be fully governed by COMP token holders.

Pros and cons of Compound Finance

Earning interest is a simple use case, and the Compound user experience is pretty intuitive. Furthermore, Compound can also be a valuable tool available to more advanced traders to increase leverage on a position.

As an example, suppose a trader is long on ETH, and they supply this ETH to the Compound protocol. Afterward, they borrow USDT against the provided ETH and use it to buy more ETH. If the price of ETH goes up and the earnings are higher than the interest paid on the loan, they make a profit.

However, this also increases the risks. If the price of ETH falls, the trader will still have to repay the borrowed amount with interest, and the ETH they provided as collateral could be liquidated.

Compound has been verified by organizations such as Trail of Bits and OpenZeppelin. While they are considered reputable auditors, bugs and vulnerabilities are part of any software and can bring unexpected problems.

You should carefully consider all risks before sending funds to a smart contract. However, regardless of the type of financial product, you should never risk funds that you cannot afford to lose. Compound is one of the most popular borrowing and lending solutions in DeFi. As many other products integrate its smart contracts into their applications, Compound will become an even more integral part of the DeFi ecosystem.

When governance becomes fully decentralized, Compound could strengthen its position in DeFi as one of the key money market protocols.

We love Compound and we use it regularly to hedge our positions by borrowing funds and using them to short our long positions and vice versa.

58

Chapter 6 - Basic Attention Token (BAT)

Up to this point, we have talked about DeFi projects. However, there are ERC-20 tokens that have nothing to do with decentralized finance and Basic Attention Token is one of those.

Designed by one of the best minds on the web, Brendan Eich, creator of Javascript and co-founder of Mozilla.org, Basic Attention Token tackles one of the biggest problems in the digital world: advertising.

BAT aims to reward users and content creators on the web based on the attention they have. The token is distributed to users based on their online activity and according to the following they attract. The BAT token can also be used to buy advertising space.

What Basic Attention Token really is

BAT is an ERC-20 token with the aim of rewarding both users and advertisers. Users watch ads and are paid accordingly. On the other hand, creators are rewarded for the amount of user attention they attract. BAT is a way to monetize attention in what many describe as "the attention economy."

BAT's reward feature is only available on the privacy-focused web browser Brave. Brave blocks third-party ads and trackers by default, and has native integration with Tor. BAT is also used to buy advertising space and reward content creators on Brave.

While you don't need Brave to trade BAT, you can take advantage of the token's features using Brave. Either way, if you just want to trade or hold it, you can do it on Binance or Coinbase.

How Basic Attention Token works

After downloading Brave, users can participate in Brave Rewards to earn BAT using the browser.

How can they do it? By using Brave and viewing advertisements. Creators are rewarded based on the attention their content attracts. Users can send BATs to their favorite content creators. Advertisers can spend BAT for a portion of users' screen space.

BAT transfers via Brave Rewards are made using the Uphold platform. This means that Uphold covers the transaction costs.

Identity verification is not required to activate and use Brave Rewards. However, if you want to withdraw your earnings or deposit more than $1000 on the platform, you will need to provide KYC information.

The importance of BAT

BAT is designed to address the problems that online advertising has failed to solve in the ongoing transition from desktop to mobile. While websites are now designed for an optimal mobile experience, the same is not always true for advertisements, which can significantly slow down your browser.

According to estimates, ads cost mobile users up to $23 a month in data in 2018, and drained up to 21% of the battery. Furthermore, advertisements can be an unwelcome distraction for many users, and it often leads to privacy violations.

On the other hand, traditional creators are losing advertising revenue due to the current state of the browser advertising landscape. Brave aims to introduce a new system that is more satisfying for all parties involved.

Basic Attention Token use cases

Advertisers can buy advertising space on Brave using BAT instead of fiat currencies. Just like on the advertising platforms of Google, Facebook and others, they can see parameters such as views, clicks, conversions and much more.

Another important use case concerns metadata. It's no secret that metadata is extremely valuable information. However, the users who generate such data usually receive nothing in return. Brave and BAT aim to reward users for their private metadata.

Individuals or organizations with websites, articles, YouTube channels, or Twitch accounts can sign up as content creators. By doing so, users can submit BATs if they wish to reward them. This type of model could create a more favorable space for rewarding the most useful content on the web.

Storing Basic Attention Token

BAT is stored in the Uphold wallet within the Brave browser. As of December 2020, this is the only place you can transfer your BAT earnings from Brave Rewards. As we mentioned earlier, if you want to withdraw your earnings from Uphold, you will need to provide KYC information.

BAT is an ERC-20 token on the Ethereum blockchain, so there are many ways to store it. Among these you will find exchanges such as Binance, web and mobile wallets, or hardware wallets. Both Ledger and Trezor support BAT.

Progress towards a more transparent blockchain-based advertising model represents a win for users, creators, and even advertising companies. Is Brave a Better Way to Advertise on the Web? Maybe. BAT has a lot of room for growth if more people participate in Brave Rewards and more companies make use of its advertising features.

We regularly invest in BAT and we have accumulated a lot of tokens around $0.2. We will hold it at least until 2022.

Chapter 7 - Swipe (SXP)

As part of the growing decentralized finance ecosystem, Swipe offers its users a wide range of products and services. Swipe's Visa debit card and multi-asset DeFi App allow you to make instant conversions between cryptocurrencies, fiat currencies and stablecoins.

As of April 2021, the app supports four stablecoins (USDT, USDC, BUSD and DAI) and two fiat currencies (USD and EUR). Currently, Swipe's Visa debit card is available in Europe, and will soon arrive in the United States as well.

All Swipe products are valued by the native SXP token, which acts as a decentralized digital currency. This native currency plays several roles in the Swipe ecosystem. Several of these reward token holders, who also present a decreasing offer over time through coin burn events.

While many DeFi tokens are considered to be speculative in nature, SXP primarily serves as a utility token in the entire Swipe ecosystem. By providing utility to token holders, there are several incentives to use or keep SXP.

A central aspect of the Swipe ecosystem is its Visa debit card. It is not the first nor the only crypto debit card in existence. However, unlike similar projects, users don't have to stake SXP in order to use the credit card service.

There are a few different versions of the Swipe debit card. While owning SXP isn't a requirement, SXP token holders can get higher-rank cards. These cards include benefits, such as Netflix or Spotify memberships, zero foreign transaction fees, and discounts with Starbucks, Uber, Apple Music, and Airbnb.

The accessible benefits depend on SXP reserves currently staking in the native mobile application.

Store SXP

Like most DeFi projects in the current crypto market, Swipe does not have a native blockchain. The team decided to issue SXP tokens on the Ethereum and Binance Chain blockchains.

Swipe Token (SXP) is available both as an ERC-20 token (on Ethereum) and as a BEP-2 token (on Binance Chain). Hence, you can easily store SXP in any crypto wallet that supports ERC-20 or BEP-2 tokens.

The offer and issue of SXP

The Swipe team has decided to limit SXP's maximum supply to 300 million tokens. However, coin burn events will gradually reduce the total supply until 100 million tokens remain.

A portion of the total offering is distributed to SXP users around the world. In addition to this, the offer changes regularly, as described below:

- 600,000 SXPs assigned each month to the company's operations.

- 10,000,000 SXPs available annually to the Swipe team and founders.

- 1,200,000 SXPs available each month for rewards in the ecosystem, including staking and other incentives.

Based on these numbers, it appears that SXP's outstanding supply will increase until it goes parabolic. However, that is not the case. In fact, the developers have decided to make SXP a deflationary asset. Tokens will be destroyed through coin burn as network usage increases.

To be more precise, 80% of the transaction fees on Swipe's network are destroyed by the smart contract. The remaining 20% of the fees remain part of the ecosystem. According to the team, this sum will eventually be distributed among the network validators, who will earn SXP for providing important services to the network.

As already mentioned, the token burns will continue until a total supply of 100,000,000 SXP is reached. From that point forward, there will be no further reductions in the offer. All commissions collected by the network will be distributed among the validators.

What is SXP used for?

The first use case is payments. The SXP asset can be used to pay at over 60 million outlets around the world. This service is possible through merchants who accept cryptocurrencies or the Swipe Visa card. In terms of transactions, SXP can be moved to both Ethereum and Binance Chain, making it a valuable asset for peer-to-peer transfers.

The second benefit is that owners receive various commission discounts. SXP owners can use their tokens to pay for transaction costs on the Swipe network, including transfers made between Swipe Wallet and Swipe's Visa card.

Another use case arises when you use Swipe's Visa debit card. With its four different ranks, there are incentives to hold or buy SXP. The larger the sum, the higher the rank of the card.

Owning SXP can introduce additional cardholder benefits, including shopping discounts and free memberships to popular streaming services. Users who stake 30,000 SXPs for six months will also be entitled to 8% cashback on all purchases and other extra benefits.

Staking users can receive SXP rewards in exchange for their contribution to protecting the network. Finally, SXP owners will be able to participate in network governance, create proposals and vote for protocol changes that affect the Swipe network.

The Swipe ecosystem includes many different products and services, and they all use the SXP token in one way or another. With its Visa debit card, Swipe is trying to make cryptocurrencies more useful and accessible for the average Joe.

Along with the deflationary model of this token, there are several reasons to take a closer look at the whitepaper and follow the evolution of the project.

We have invested in SXP in June 2020 and we averaged down our entry price during October and November. As cryptocurrency sees mainstream adoption, we believe this company is going to do very well.

Chapter 8 - Uniswap (UNI)

For years, centralized exchanges have been the backbone of the cryptocurrency market. They offer fast settlement times, high trading volume and continuously improving liquidity. However, there is a parallel world built in the form of trustless protocols. Decentralized exchanges do not require any intermediary or depositary to facilitate trading.

Due to the inherent limitations of blockchain technology, it was difficult to create a decentralized exchange that could truly compete with their centralized counterparts. Most DEXs need improvements in both performance and user experience.

Many developers are thinking of new ways to build a decentralized exchange. One of the pioneers in this situation is Uniswap. How Uniswap works may be more difficult to understand than a more traditional DEX. However, you will soon see that this model introduces some interesting advantages.

Thanks to this innovation, Uniswap has become one of the most successful projects within the decentralized finance movement.

Let's take a look at what Uniswap is, how it works and how you can use it to simply trade tokens with an Ethereum wallet.

What is Uniswap?

Uniswap is a decentralized exchange protocol developed on Ethereum. To be more precise, it is an automated liquidity protocol. There are no order books and no centralized participants are required to trade. Uniswap allows users to trade without intermediaries, with a high degree of decentralization and resistance to censorship.

Uniswap is an open-source software. You can check out its code on Uniswap's GitHub page.

Uniswap works according to a model that involves the creation of liquidity pools by liquidity providers. This system provides a decentralized pricing mechanism that basically rounds the depth of the order book. Soon we will see how it works in detail. For now, just know that users can trade ERC-20 tokens directly without the need for an order book.

Since the Uniswap protocol is decentralized, it has no listing process. In practice, any ERC-20 token can be listed as long as there is a liquidity pool available for traders. Consequently,

Uniswap does not charge any listing fees. In a sense, the Uniswap protocol acts as a kind of public service.

The Uniswap protocol was created in 2018 by Hayden Adams, but the underlying technology that inspired its implementation was first described by Ethereum co-founder Vitalik Buterin.

How Uniswap works

Uniswap leaves behind the traditional architecture of digital exchanges, as it does not have an order book. It works according to a design called the Constant Product Market Maker, a variant of a model known as the Automated Market Maker.

AMMs, also called automated market makers, are smart contracts that contain liquidity reserves against which it is possible to trade. These reserves are financed by liquidity providers. Anyone can be a liquidity provider by depositing an equivalent value of two tokens in the pool. In return, traders pay a commission to the pool which is then distributed to liquidity providers based on their share of the pool. Let's examine how this process works in more detail.

Liquidity providers create a market by depositing an equivalent value of two assets, be it ETH and an ERC-20 token or two ERC-20 tokens. Often these pools are made up of stablecoins like DAI, USDC or USDT, but that's not a requirement. In return, liquidity providers receive "liquidity tokens," which represent their share of the entire pool. These liquidity tokens can be redeemed for the share they represent in the pool.

Let's consider the ETH/USDT liquidity pool. We will call the ETH portion of the pool x and the USDT portion y. Uniswap takes these two quantities and multiplies them to calculate the total liquidity in the pool, which we will call k. The idea behind Uniswap is that k must remain constant. Therefore the total liquidity in the pool is constant. The formula for total liquidity in the pool is: $x * y = k$

Trading on Uniswap

Suppose Alice buys 1ETH for 300USDT using the ETH/USDT liquidity pool. By doing so, it increases the USDT portion and reduces the ETH portion of the pool. This actually means that the price of ETH goes up. Why? Because there are fewer ETHs in the pool following the transaction, and we know that total liquidity (k) must remain constant. This mechanism is what determines the prices. Ultimately, the price paid for this ETH is based on how much a given trade shifts the ratio between x and y.

It should be noted that this model does not scale linearly. In fact, the larger the order, the more it will shift the balance between x and y. This means that larger orders become exponentially more expensive than smaller orders, leading to increasingly larger slippage. It also implies that the larger a liquidity pool, the easier it will be to place large orders. Why? Because in that case, the shift between x and y will be smaller.

Impermanent loss

As we have already mentioned, liquidity providers earn commission for providing liquidity to traders who can trade between tokens. Is there anything else liquidity providers should pay attention to? Yes, an effect called impermanent loss.

Suppose Alice deposits 1 ETH and 100 USDT in an Uniswap pool. Since the token pair must have equivalent value, this means that the price of ETH is 100 USDT. At the same time, there are a total of 10 ETH and 1,000 USDT in the pool. The rest was provided by other liquidity providers such as Alice. This means that Alice has a 10% share of the pool. In this case, the total liquidity (k) is 10,000.

What happens if the price of ETH reaches 400 USDT? Remember, the total liquidity in the pool must remain constant. If ETH is now at 400 USDT, the ratio of the amount of ETH to the amount of USDT in the pool has changed. In fact, there are now 5 ETH and 2,000 USDT in the pool. Traders taking advantage of the arbitrage opportunity will add USDT to the pool and remove ETH from it as long as the ratio reflects the correct price. For this reason it is essential to understand that k is constant.

Then, Alice decides to withdraw her funds and receives 10% of the pool according to her share. As a result, she receives 0.5 ETH and 200 USDT, for a total of 400 USDT. Looks like she made a nice profit. But wait a minute, what would have happened if she hadn't deposited her funds into the pool? She would now have 1 ETH and 100 USDT, for a total of 500 USDT.

In fact, Alice would have done better just by holding the coins, instead of depositing them into the Uniswap pool. In this case, the impermanent loss is essentially the opportunity cost associated with pooling a token whose price increases. Simply by depositing funds into Uniswap in hopes of earning commissions, Alice may be missing out on other opportunities. Please remember that this effect occurs regardless of the direction of price movements following the deposit. If the price of ETH decreases from the time of deposit, the losses could also be amplified.

If the price of the tokens added to the pool returns to the price corresponding to the time they were added, the effect is canceled. Additionally, as liquidity providers earn commissions, the loss could be offset over time. However, liquidity providers need to understand this before adding funds to a pool.

How does Uniswap generate profits?

Simple, it doesn't. All commissions go to liquidity providers, and none of the founders get a slice from the trades that happen through the protocol.

Currently, the transaction cost paid to liquidity providers is 0.3% per transaction. By default, these fees are added to the liquidity pool, but suppliers can redeem them at any time. Fees are distributed based on each liquidity provider's share of the pool.

In the future, a portion of the commissions could be dedicated to the development of Uniswap. The Uniswap team has already implemented an improved version of the protocol called Uniswap v2.

Chapter 9 - A Deeper Look at Impermanent Loss

In the previous chapter we have briefly talked about this concept. However, we feel there is the need for more clarity and we have decided to get a bit deeper into this concept.

Impermanent loss occurs when the price of your tokens changes from the time you deposited them into the pool. The greater the variation, the greater the loss.

DeFi protocols such as Uniswap, SushiSwap or PancakeSwap have seen an explosion in volume and liquidity. These liquidity protocols allow virtually anyone who owns funds to become a market maker and earn trading fees. The democratization of market making has allowed for a lot of frictionless economic activity in the crypto sector.

An explanation of impermanent loss

As mentioned before, impermanent loss occurs when you provide liquidity to a liquidity pool, and the price of the assets you provide changes from the time you deposited them. The greater this change, the more exposed you are to impermanent loss. In this case, the loss means less dollar value at the withdrawal than the value at the time of the deposit.

Pools containing assets that remain in a relatively narrow price range will be less exposed to permanent loss. Different stablecoins or wrapped versions of a coin, for example, will remain in a relatively limited price range. In this case, there is a much lower risk of impermanent loss for liquidity providers.

Why do liquidity providers continue to provide liquidity if they are exposed to this risk? Well, the impermanent loss can be offset by trading fees. In fact, even the pools on Uniswap exposed to impermanent losses can prove to be profitable thanks to trading fees.

Uniswap charges a 0.3% commission on each transaction, a cost that goes directly to the liquidity providers. If a given pool has a high trading volume, it can be profitable to provide liquidity to it even if the pool is heavily exposed to impermanent loss.

However, this depends on the protocol, the specific pool, the deposited assets and even the general market conditions.

How does impermanent loss happen?

Let's look at an example of what impermanent loss might look like for a liquidity provider.

Alice deposits 1 ETH and 100 DAI in a liquidity pool. In this particular automated market maker (AMM), the deposited token pair must have an equivalent value. This means that the price of ETH is 100 DAI at the time of deposit. Therefore, the dollar value of Alice's deposit equals 200 USD to the deposit.

In the pool we find a total of 10 ETH and 1,000 DAI. These are provided by other LPs just like Alice. Therefore, Alice has a 10% stake in the pool, and the total liquidity is 10,000.

Suppose the price of ETH rises to 400 DAI. As this happens, traders taking advantage of the arbitrage opportunity will add DAI to the pool and remove ETH from it as long as the ratio reflects the current price. Remember, AMMs have no order books. What determines the price of the assets in the pool is the ratio of the two in the pool. While liquidity remains constant, the ratio of assets within it changes.

If ETH is now worth 400 DAI, the ratio between the amount of ETH and DAI in the pool has changed. There are now 5 ETH and 2,000 DAI in the pool, thanks to traders' arbitrage.

Therefore, Alice decides to withdraw her funds. As we mentioned earlier, you are entitled to a 10% stake in the pool. As a result, you can withdraw 0.5 ETH and 200 DAI, for a total of 400 USD. She has made considerable profits as her token deposit was worth 200 USD, right? But what if she just holded her 1 ETH and 100 DAI in a wallet, the combined dollar value of these assets would now be $500.

We can see that Alice would have done better by holding instead of depositing into a cash pool. This is what we call impermanent loss. In this case, Alice's impermanent loss is not that serious as the initial deposit was a relatively small sum. Remember that impermanent loss can lead to large losses. Be careful with liquidity pools.

That said, Alice's example completely ignores the trading fees she would have earned for providing liquidity. In many cases, the commissions earned make it possible to recover losses and make the process profitable. Either way, it is vital to understand the concept of impermanent loss before providing liquidity to a DeFi protocol.

Calculating the impermanent loss

You know that impermanent loss occurs when the price of the assets in the pool changes.

Here is a summary of what the impermanent loss is for different changes in price.

- 1.25x price change = loss of 0.6%

- 1.50x price change = loss of 2.0%

- 1.75x price change = loss of 3.8%

- 2x price change = 5.7% loss

- 3x price change = 13.4% loss

- 4x price change = loss of 20.0%

- 5x price change = 25.5% loss

There is another important factor to keep in mind. The impermanent loss occurs regardless of the direction of price changes. The only thing that concerns the impermanent loss is the relationship of the price to the time of the deposit.

The risks associated with providing liquidity to an AMM

It is called an impermanent loss because losses only happen when you withdraw your coins from the liquidity pool. At that point, the loss becomes permanent. The fees you earn may be able to offset these losses, but it remains a slightly misleading name.

Be very careful when depositing funds into an AMM. As we have mentioned, some liquidity pools are much more exposed to impermanent loss than others. Generally speaking, the more volatile the assets in the pool, the more likely you are to be exposed to permanent loss. Furthermore, it may be a better move to start by depositing a small amount. This way, you can get a rough estimate of the returns you can expect before committing a more significant part of your capital.

One final consideration has to be made. Please, only use the most tried and tested AMMs. DeFi makes it pretty easy to fork an existing AMM and add small changes to it. However, this could expose you to bugs, potentially blocking your liquidity forever. If a liquidity pool promises unusually high returns, perhaps there is a trade-off somewhere, and the associated risks are likely higher as well.

Impermanent loss is one of the fundamental concepts that anyone wishing to provide liquidity to AMMs should understand.We advise you to read this chapter a couple of times and familiarize with this concept, before exploring the possibilities provided by liquidity pools.

Chapter 10 - SushiSwap

Uniswap is one of the most successful DeFi protocols for token exchange on Ethereum. It was created by a small team of passionate developers who have made the code open-source and available to anyone interested in a fork. And that's exactly what SushiSwap did.

SushiSwap is a fork of Uniswap that adds the SUSHI token to it. It gives holders control over the protocol and distributes a portion of the commissions to them. Let's see how it works.

As Decentralized Finance evolves, new financial platforms continue to emerge. We will see how flash loans and yield farming can be used by investors to make money by putting their funds to work.

Uniswap has solidified its position as one of DeFi's core protocols. However, despite its decentralized ethos and heavy reliance on smart contracts, users don't have much say in the direction of development.

SushiSwap, a newcomer to the industry, has decided to change that. A few days after its launch, the protocol boasted over $1 billion in locked value, suggesting that many were interested in this change.

What is SushiSwap?

SushiSwap is a fork of Uniswap with some key differences. The most notable one is the SUSHI token. This token has two functions: to give holders governance rights and a portion of the fees paid to the protocol. In a simplified way, SUSHI holders "own" the protocol.

Why has this aroused such interest? Because Community governance is strongly intertwined with the DeFi philosophy. The growth of liquidity mining as a viable method for token distribution has resulted in a large number of new token launches. These events aim to level the playing field for all attendees, with no pre-mines, little or no founder allocations, and fair distribution based on the amount of funds provided. Tokens distributed through these liquidity incentives confer governance rights on holders. Furthermore, we already know that SUSHI holders receive a share of the commissions paid by traders for using the protocol.

Anyone can submit a SushiSwap Improvement Proposal (SIP), which SUSHI holders will later vote on with their tokens. They can be minor or major changes to the SushiSwap protocol. Instead of a more traditional team like that of Uniswap, the development of SushiSwap is in the hands of the SUSHI token holders. A strong community can be an important asset to any project in this area, but this is especially true for a DeFi protocol.

Uniswap vs. SushiSwap

It is no secret that cryptocurrencies are deeply rooted in the spirit of open-source code. Many believe that Bitcoin and an increasing number of permissionless DeFi protocols are acting as new forms of public goods in the form of software. As these designs are easily copied and relaunched with minor modifications, it is natural for competition to arise between similar products. However, it could be assumed that this phenomenon ultimately leads to better products for the end user.

Without a doubt, many significant advances in the DeFi industry are attributable to the Uniswap team. However, we could imagine a future in which both Uniswap and SushiSwap can thrive. Uniswap could remain at the forefront of innovation within the AMMs, while SushiSwap could provide a more focused alternative on the features the community wants.

That said, fragmenting liquidity across similar protocols is not ideal. If you've read our chapter on Uniswap, you'll know that AMMs work best with as much liquidity as possible in pools. If much of the liquidity in DeFi is split across different AMM protocols, it could lead to a worse end-user experience.

The distribution of SUSHI rewards

SUSHI tokens are distributed to those who provide liquidity to specific Uniswap pools. Afterward, they can deposit their Uniswap LP tokens into SushiSwap's staking contracts to start earning SUSHI.

Initially, these Uniswap pools were the following.

● USDT-ETH

- USDC-ETH

- DAI-ETH

- sUSD-ETH

- COMP-ETH

- LEND-ETH

- SNX-ETH

- UMA-ETH

- LINK-ETH

- BAND-ETH

- AMPL-ETH

- YFI-ETH

- SUSHI-ETH

To incentivize the provision of liquidity for the SUSHI market, the SUSHI-ETH pool distributed double rewards. Shortly after the launch, SUSHI owners voted to add additional pools to participate in the distribution. This showed the power of community governance.

The distribution of SUSHI rewards began from the 10,750,000 block of Ethereum. Rewards were reduced after 100,000 blocks. After this initial distribution period, the liquidity tokens in the staking contract were migrated to SushiSwap contracts. This means that all Uniswap LP tokens staking on SushiSwap were redeemed on Uniswap for the tokens they represented, and were used to create new liquidity pools on SushiSwap. This event effectively marked the launch of the SushiSwap exchange.

Is SushiSwap Safe?

At the time of writing, SushiSwap is an unverified project. Depositing funds in a smart contract always carries the risk of bugs, even for verified and reliable projects. However, SushiSwap was created by anonymous developers, which makes depositing funds even more risky.

SushiSwap is a fun experiment, but never deposit more than you can afford to lose. Also, due to the extremely high fees on Ethereum, smaller deposits may need to do a lot of farming before they can make a profit.

That said, SushiSwap developers have invited several accounting firms to review their smart contracts. SushiSwap is an interesting experiment that challenges the competitive advantage of Uniswap.

The real SushiSwap test began after the initial two-week distribution period ended. We must say that it is doing pretty well right now and we are providing some liquidity to its pools. Furthermore, we have also invested in its token.

Chapter 11 - Security Tokens

A security is a financial instrument that has value and can be traded. Under this definition, many of the instruments we see today - stocks, bonds, options - could be considered securities.

In a legal context, the definition is considerably more subtle, and varies from jurisdiction to jurisdiction. If an instrument is considered a security according to the criteria of a certain country, it will be subject to heavy regulatory scrutiny.

In this chapter, we will discuss how blockchain technology is going to optimize traditional financial markets with security tokens.

What is a security token?

A security token is a token, issued on a blockchain, which represents a share in some business or external asset. These tokens can be issued by entities such as companies or governments and serve the same purpose as their outgoing counterparts (i.e. stocks, bonds, etc.).

Use cases

To make an example, suppose a company intends to distribute shares to investors in tokenized form. These tokens can be designed to provide the same benefits that would be expected from shares - specifically, voting rights and dividends.

The benefits of this approach are numerous. As with cryptocurrencies and other forms of tokens, security tokens benefit from the properties of the blockchain on which they are issued. These properties include transparency, quick settlement, no downtime, and divisibility.

Transparency

On a public ledger, the identities of the participants are anonymous, but everything else can be verified. Anyone is free to examine the smart contracts that manage the tokens, or monitor the issuance and properties.

Quick settlement

Clearing and settlement have long been seen as a bottleneck in the context of asset transfers. While operations can be done almost instantly, reassigning ownership often takes time. On a blockchain, the process is automated and can be completed in minutes.

Times of activity

Existing financial markets are somewhat limited in their uptime. They are open for fixed periods of time on weekdays, and closed on weekends. On the other hand, digital asset markets are active at any time, every day of the year.

Severability

Works of art, real estate and other high-value assets, once tokenized, may be accessible to investors who may not otherwise be able to invest. For example, we could have a painting worth $5M tokenized in 5,000 units, so that each is worth $1,000. This would greatly increase accessibility.

However, it should be noted that some security tokens may have a limit in terms of divisibility. In some cases, if voting or dividend rights are conferred as a share, there may be a limit on the divisibility of the token for execution purposes.

Security token vs. utility token

Security tokens and utility tokens have many similarities. Technically, the offerings in both groups are identical. They are managed by smart contracts, can be sent to blockchain addresses, and are traded on exchanges or through peer-to-peer transactions.

The differences between the two mainly concern the economy and the regulations that support them. They can be issued in Initial Coin Offering (ICO) or Initial Exchange Offering (IEO), so that startups or consolidated projects can co-finance the development of their ecosystems.

By contributing funds, users receive these digital tokens, which allow participation in the project network. They can confer voting rights on the holder, or serve as a protocol-specific currency to access products or services.

Utility tokens have no intrinsic value. If a project grows and succeeds, investors are not entitled to any portion of the profits, as is the case with some traditional securities. We could compare the role of tokens to loyalty points. They can be used to buy goods, but they offer no stake in the company that distributes them.

Consequently, their value is often due to speculation. Many investors buy tokens in the hope that the price will rise as the ecosystem develops. If the project fails, there is very little protection for the owner.

Security tokens are issued in a similar way to utility tokens, even though the distribution event is called a Security Token Offering (STO). However, from an investment perspective, the two types of tokens represent completely different instruments.

Even if issued on a blockchain, security tokens remain securities. As such, they are heavily regulated to protect investors and prevent fraud. In this sense, an STO is much more like an IPO than an ICO.

Generally speaking, when investors buy a security token, they are buying stocks, bonds or derivatives. Their tokens effectively act as investment contracts and grant ownership rights to off-chain assets.

What makes a token a security?

At present, the blockchain sector does not have the necessary legal clarity. Regulators around the world are still trying to catch up with a wave of new financial technologies. There have been instances where issuers believed they had issued utility tokens, which were later declared security by the Securities and Exchange Commission (SEC).

Perhaps the most famous parameter for trying to determine whether a transaction corresponds to an 'investment contract' is the Howey Test. In short, it seeks to establish whether an individual investing in a joint venture expects to profit from the promoter's actions.

The test was produced by US courts long before the arrival of blockchain technology. Therefore, it is difficult to apply it to the myriad of new tokens. That said, it remains a popular tool among regulators looking to categorize digital assets.

Obviously, each jurisdiction will have a different regulatory framework, but many follow a similar logic.

Security token and programmable finance

Considering the current size of the markets, tokenization could radically transform the traditional financial world. Investors and institutions in the sector would benefit enormously from a fully digital approach to financial instruments.

Over the years, a centralized database ecosystem has created a great deal of friction. Institutions must devote resources to administrative processes to manage external data incompatible with their systems. The lack of industry-wide standardization increases costs for businesses and delays settlement considerably.

A blockchain is a shared database that any user or company can easily interact with. Functions previously handled by institutions' servers could now be outsourced to a registry used by the rest of the industry. By tokenizing the securities, we can connect them to an interoperable network, allowing fast settlement times and global compatibility.

After that, automation can handle processes that would otherwise take a long time. For example, KYC / AML compliance, blocking of investments for set periods of time, and many other functions can be handled by code running on the blockchain.

Security tokens appear to be a logical progression for the financial sector. Despite their use of blockchain technology, they are much closer to traditional securities than to cryptocurrencies or other tokens.

However, work remains to be done on the regulatory front. With assets that can be easily moved around the world, authorities need to find effective ways to regulate their issuance and flow. Some speculated that this can be automated with smart contracts that encode certain rules. Projects such as Ravencoin, Liquid and Polymath already facilitate the issuance of security tokens.

If the promise of security tokens were to materialize, the operations of financial institutions could be significantly optimized. Over time, the use of blockchain-based tokens in place of traditional tools could very well catalyze the merger between legacy and cryptocurrency markets.

Chapter 12 - Bringing Bitcoin on Ethereum

Now that we have a good understanding of what the blockchain is and how tokens work, we can dive deeper into more complicated topics. Before considering other protocols, like Cardano, Polkadot or Flare, we need to discuss how Bitcoin can be implemented on other blockchains. In particular, in this chapter we will see how Bitcoin can be wrapped on ETH.

Typically, Bitcoin is seen as a "reserve asset" or store of value in the cryptocurrency industry. As a result, it has the highest adoption, the best liquidity, the highest average trading volume and is the first crypto in terms of market capitalization. In fact, some believe that there is no need for other cryptocurrencies besides Bitcoin, as it could satisfy all the use cases that altcoins are aimed at.

Either way, blockchain technology is thriving in many different segments. The decentralized finance movement aims to bring financial applications to the blockchain. These decentralized applications (dApps) run on public and permissionless networks, making trustless financial transactions possible without the need for a central coordinator. While the DeFi concept is independent of a specific blockchain, and can run on any smart contract platform, most of the business is currently on Ethereum.

Bitcoin is the backbone of the cryptocurrency market, yet it cannot take advantage of developments taking place in other parts of the ecosystem. Some projects are working to solve this problem.

How can we use bitcoin for more than it can currently do while keeping the Bitcoin network intact? Well, the growth of tokenized bitcoins on Ethereum suggests some demand for this application.

What is a Tokenized Bitcoin?

Before we begin, there is something we need to clarify to avoid confusion. By now, you know that Bitcoin written with a capital letter indicates the network, while bitcoin written with a lowercase is the unit of account.

The idea behind bitcoin tokenization is relatively simple. The process consists of blocking BTC through some mechanism, issuing tokens on another network and using BTC as a token on it. Each token on the other network represents a specific amount of bitcoin. The anchoring between the two assets should be maintained, and the process should be reversible. In other words, you can destroy these tokens to unlock the "original" bitcoins on the Bitcoin blockchain again.

In the case of Ethereum, this means ERC-20 tokens representing bitcoin. By doing so, users can carry out bitcoin-denominated transactions on the Ethereum network. Furthermore, through this process it is possible to make bitcoins programmable - like any other token on Ethereum.
You can check the current total amount of tokenized bitcoins on Ethereum by visiting btconethereum.com.

As of April 2021, we count around 30,000 tokenized BTCs on Ethereum. That might sound like a lot, but it's a tiny number compared to the ~ 18.5 million supply in circulation. However, this may just be the beginning.

It is important to note that sidechains and Layer 2 solutions like Bitcoin's Lightning Network or Liquid Network also aim to solve similar challenges. There are currently over ten times as many bitcoins on Ethereum as in Bitcoin's Lightning Network.
However, the competition between these different solutions is not that simple. It is not a zero-sum game. In fact, many believe

they are complementary, not adversary. Tokenization projects could increase the options available to bitcoin holders, while tokenless projects improve the overall infrastructure. This could result in greater integration within this domain, which in turn would benefit the entire sector.

The importance of having Bitcoin on Ethereum

Bitcoin's design is intentionally simple. It was designed to do a few things very well. However, these properties have inherent limitations.

While most of the value lies in Bitcoin, its network cannot benefit much from the innovation taking place in other segments of the digital currency industry. It is technically possible to run smart contracts on Bitcoin, but the functionality is quite limited compared to Ethereum or other smart contract platforms.

Tokenizing bitcoin on other blockchains could increase the usefulness of the network. In fact, it might allow for features that aren't natively supported on Bitcoin. At the same time, Bitcoin's core functionality and security model remain intact. Additional benefits could be higher transaction speeds, fungibility and privacy.

Furthermore, one of the most important aspects of DeFi is the concept of composability. Since all of these applications operate on the same public, open-source, and permissionless base layer, they can work perfectly with each other.

Bringing Bitcoin to this composable entry level of financial modules is considered by many to be an exciting prospect. It could give birth to a large number of new applications that use bitcoin and would not otherwise be possible.

The tokenization process

There are many ways to tokenize Bitcoin on Ethereum and other blockchains. Each has varying degrees of decentralization and different assumptions about trust and risk.

The two main types of tokenization process can be defined as custodial and non-custodial. The first concerns a centralized depository, which could also deal with the issue of the tokens. This method introduces counterparty risk, as it is necessary to trust the entity that holds the bitcoins. However, this implementation could be considered safer than the alternatives.

The other solution is a bit different. There is no need for reliable entities, as the entire issue and burn process is performed by automated on-chain processes. Collateral assets are blocked, and tokens issued on the other blockchain through certain on-chain mechanisms. Funds remain on-chain until they are unlocked with the destruction of the tokens. While this method eliminates counterparty risks, it increases the potential security risks. Why? Because in this case, the burden of risk rests entirely on the shoulders of the user. In the event of a user or contract error that leads to a loss of funds, they are likely lost forever.

Examples of tokenized Bitcoin

Custodial solutions

These solutions represent a significant portion of the current amount of tokenized bitcoins. The largest locked value is found in Wrapped Bitcoin (WBTC). Users send bitcoins to a centralized depository that stores them in a multi-signature cold storage wallet, and issues WBTC tokens in return. The process requires identity verification to comply with KYC / AML regulations. This method requires trust in the entity issuing the token, but at the same time offers security benefits.

Binance also has a tokenized version of BTC called BTCB. It is a BEP-2 token issued on Binance Chain. If you want to try it, visit Binance DEX.

Non custodial

Non-custodial solutions work completely on-chain, without any involvement of centralized custodians. Simply put, you can see them as similar to Wrapped BTC, but instead of a centralized depository, they feature a smart contract or virtual machine that keeps the funds safe and issues the tokens. Users can deposit BTC and receive tokenized bitcoins through a trustless and permissionless process.

Some of these systems require overcollateralization meaning users have to deposit more collateral value than they intend to issue. In this way, the system can prepare for black swan events and major market crashes. However, if the value of the collateral decreases significantly, these systems may not be able to address such scenarios.

The most popular non-custodial implementation is renBTC. Bitcoins are sent to the Ren Virtual Machine, which stores them using a network of decentralized nodes. It issues ERC-20 tokens based on the amount of bitcoins sent.

Other notable examples are sBTC and iBTC, synthetic tokens backed by Synthetix Network Token instead of bitcoin. What makes iBTC particularly interesting is the fact that it inversely tracks the price of Bitcoin, offering one of the few non-custodial methods to short Bitcoin.

Importantly, these are highly experimental technologies. No wonder custodial and centralized solutions are more popular these days. In fact, they tend to be more secure. Of course, there is also a greater risk of bugs and user error, which can potentially lead to loss of funds. Either way, these innovations could be the future of tokenization once the technology is improved.

Since these non-custodial solutions are governed by automated processes, their use is only recommended for experienced users. If you want to test these tokens without worrying about the issuing process, you can buy and trade them on cryptocurrency exchanges.

The advantages for Bitcoin

Tokenization undoubtedly increases Bitcoin's usefulness. While many argue that Bitcoin doesn't necessarily need more functionality, a little bit of would come in handy. As we mentioned earlier, the benefits can include higher transaction speeds, fungibility, privacy, and lower transaction costs. With the launch of ETH 2.0, we can expect Ethereum transactions to be faster and cheaper. This could support the use case of bitcoin tokenization on Ethereum as well.

On the other hand, some say that this practice is potentially dangerous for holders of tokenized bitcoins. Tokenization of BTC involves giving up the important security benefits of Bitcoin, which is one of its most fundamental properties.

For example, what happens if tokenized bitcoins are stolen or lost due to a bug in the smart contract? There may not be a way to unlock BTCs locked on the Bitcoin blockchain.

Another aspect to consider is the fees. Some argue that if many users started using the Ethereum blockchain to transfer tokenized BTC, the transaction fees on the Bitcoin network would decrease. In the long run, Bitcoin will only need to be backed by fees, and if most of these pass through the Ethereum ecosystem, network security could be compromised. However, there are still several years to this stage since the number of tokenized Bitcoin is pretty low.

The advantages for Ethereum

If Ethereum acquires some of Bitcoin's value, it could consolidate itself as a global network for the transfer of value. According to research by Etherscan, a sizable portion of the 30,000 BTC previously mentioned is locked inside Ethereum's DeFi ecosystem.

Tokenized bitcoins could greatly increase DeFi's usefulness on Ethereum. In fact, financial services based on tokenized bitcoin could be created. DEXs, marketplace loans, cash pools and any other existing projects in DeFi may be denominated in BTC. The success of tokenized bitcoins could also encourage the migration of other types of assets to the Ethereum network.

Most projects are still in the very early stages of development, and the technology they are based on has a lot of room for improvement. However, there are certainly some interesting developments in the future of this sector.

If Ethereum manages to acquire a significant portion of Bitcoin transactions, there could be major implications for the future. The entire blockchain industry could benefit from building bridges between the two largest cryptocurrency networks.

Conclusion

Congratulations on making it to the end of this book, we hope you found some useful insights to take your cryptocurrency trading skills to the next level. As you should know by now, the world of cryptocurrency is extremely complicated and there is a new "opportunity" every way you look. However, our experience tells us that only by taking things seriously and having a proper plan you can develop your investing skills to the point that you can actually accumulate wealth.

Our final advice is to stay away from the shining objects that the world of cryptocurrencies offers you every day. Simply study the world of cryptocurrencies in depth and when you feel ready try to invest a little bit of money. Analyze your results, improve your money management skills and become the master of your emotions.

As you can see, there are no shortcuts you can take. Easy money does not exist. What exists is the possibility to start from zero and work your way up to become a professional cryptocurrency investor. The journey might be difficult, but it is certainly worth it.

To your success!

Bitcoin, Cryptocurrency, NFT and DeFi

The Ultimate Investing Guide to Create Generational Wealth During the 2021 Bull Run! Learn How to Take Advantage of the Opportunities provided by the Blockchain!

damages that may befall them after undertaking information described herein.

Additionally, the information in the following pages is intended only for informational purposes and should thus be thought of as universal. As befitting its nature, it is presented without assurance regarding its prolonged validity or interim quality. Trademarks that are mentioned are done without written consent and can in no way be considered an endorsement from the trademark holder.

Table of Contents

Introduction

Bitcoin has taken the world by storm once again when it crossed $20,000 per BTC in December of last year. After more than 2 years of bear market, the most famous cryptocurrency surpassed its previous all time high.

A lot of people are now trying to improvise themselves as professional investors and are losing a lot of money, only helping those who actually know what they are doing accumulate an incredible amount of wealth that will lead to generational fortunes.

To join the club of the few investors that actually make it, you need the right knowledge and the right mindset. Notice how we did not include a large initial capital. In fact, while having more money to invest means having more fire power, it is not necessary to have thousands of dollars to accumulate cryptocurrency and build wealth.

In fact, when we started investing in cryptocurrency we only had a few hundreds to put into the market, but that sum yielded us thousands and thousands of dollars over the span of a few years.

In this book you are going to discover everything there is to know about the fascinating world of cryptocurrency. From the operation of the Bitcoin blockchain to more advanced projects, like Uniswap and Compound.

If you diligently study the content of this book, we are sure you are going to see take your crypto knowledge to the next level. This also means you are going to see amazing results in a relative short period of time, since this bull run is offering an amazing number of opportunities.

To your success!

Kevin Anderson

Chapter 1 - Curve Finance (CRV)

In the previous chapter, we mentioned the Curve Finance protocol. Since it plays a fundamental role when it comes to DeFi, we believe it is important to dive a bit deeper into what it is and how it works.

Automated Market Makers have had a major impact on the crypto landscape. Liquidity protocols like Uniswap, Balancer and PancakeSwap allow anyone to become a market maker and earn commissions on many currency pairs.

Can these AMMs significantly compete with centralized exchanges? Maybe. But there is one sector of the market where they are already showing great potential and that is stablecoin trading. Curve Finance is at the forefront in this context.

What Curve Finance is

Curve Finance is an automated market maker protocol designed for trading between stablecoins with minimal fees and slippage. It is a decentralized liquidity aggregator where anyone can add assets to different liquidity pools and earn commissions.

Because of the way the pricing formula works on Curve, it can also be extremely useful for trading tokens that trade in a relatively small price range.

This means that they are not only valid for exchanges between stablecoins, but also between different tokenized versions of a coin. Hence, Curve is one of the best ways to trade different tokenized versions of Bitcoin, such as WBTC, renBTC, and sBTC.

At the time of writing, Curve is making 36 pools available to trade different stablecoins and assets. Of course, these are constantly changing based on market demand and DeFi's ever-changing landscape. Some of the more popular stablecoins available include USDT, USDC, DAI, BUSD, TUSD, and sUSD.

There is no official information relating to the Curve team, but most of the contributions on GitHub were made by Michael Egorov, the CTO of a cybersecurity company called NuCypher.

How Curve Finance works

As already mentioned, assets are priced based on a certain formula instead of an order book. The formula used by Curve is specially designed to facilitate trades that occur in an approximately similar range.

For example, we know that 1 USDT should equal 1 USDC, which in turn equals 1 BUSD, and so on. However, if you want to convert $100 million USDT to USDC, and then convert it to BUSD, you will have to contend with some slippage. Curve's formula is designed to minimize this slippage as much as possible.

One thing to take into consideration is that if these assets weren't in the same price range, the Curve formula would not work efficiently. However, the system does not take this possibility into account. After all, if USDT is worth $0.7, something else outside of Curve has gone terribly wrong. The system cannot solve things outside its control, so as long as the tokens hold their value, the formula does its job very well.

This results in extremely low slippage even for large trades. In fact, the spread on Curve can hold its own against some centralized exchanges and OTC trading desks with the best liquidity.

There are several assumptions about trust and risk, so liquidity and execution are not the full picture. However, it is undoubtedly exciting to see the competition between the centralized and the decentralized world.

The CRV token

CRV is the governance token of CurveDAO, a decentralized autonomous organization that manages the protocol. CRV is constantly distributed to the liquidity providers of the protocol, at a rate that decreases on an annual basis.

As of April 2021, each trade on the platform carries a 0.04% trading fee which is distributed directly to liquidity providers.

Risks of Curve Finance

Curve was verified by a company called Trail of Bits. However, this audit does not mean that the project is completely safe to use. When you use any smart contract, there are always risks, no matter how many audits have been done. Deposit only what you are willing to lose.

As with any other automated market maker protocol, you will need to consider impermanent loss as well.

Behind the scenes, the liquidity pool could also be provided to Compound or yearn.finance in order to generate greater income for liquidity providers. Furthermore, thanks to the magic of modularity, trading on Curve is not only reserved for users, but is available to other smart contracts as well. This introduces additional risks, as many of these DeFi protocols become dependent on each other. If one breaks, we could see a damaging chain reaction across the entire DeFi ecosystem.

Swerve Finance

Like SushiSwap and Uniswap, Curve Finance has a high profile hard fork as well. This hard fork is called Swerve Finance.

Swerve is advertised as a "fair launch," meaning that its governance token (SWRV) has not been distributed with an allocation reserved for the team or founder. SWRV tokens were distributed through a liquidity mining event, where everyone had an equal opportunity to farm them. Therefore, Swerve claims to be a 100% community-managed fork of Curve.

Curve is one of the most popular automated market makers active on Ethereum. It facilitates high-volume stablecoin trading with minimal slippage and tight spreads on a non-custodial basis.

Another feature that places Curve Finance at the heart of the DeFi industry is the fact that other blockchain protocols are highly dependent on its functions. Composability between different decentralized applications carries risks, but it is also one of the main advantages of DeFi.

When we want to go from one stablecoin to another, we always use Curve Finance, as slippage is basically non existent. We encourage you to check it out and familiarize with it before doing anything.

Chapter 2 - Alpha Homora (ALPHA)

Yield farming in the DeFi sector often involves providing liquidity to a decentralized exchange such as Uniswap. In return, users can earn a portion of the commissions generated by the trading pair they are providing liquidity to.

Alpha Homora allows you to increase your yield farming position with up to 2.5x leverage. It also allows you to earn based on your personal preferences and risk appetite. This way, you can increase your overall returns from liquidity mining. However, using leverage also increases the associated risks. Let's see how this all works.

The most successful projects in DeFi allow users to participate in yield farming by providing liquidity. Most of these initiatives are based on the Ethereum ecosystem. Binance Smart Chain also supports this type of functionality, which is why the Alpha Finance Lab team has decided to build its DeFi ecosystem on both BSC and Ethereum.

What is Alpha Homora?

Alpha Homora is the second working product developed by Alpha Finance Lab. It is designed to allow users to increase their exposure to liquidity mining. More precisely, those who participate in yield farming in DeFi can "amplify" their positions. This is probably the first case in which leverage enters the scene for yield farmers, making Alpha Homora a unique project in the decentralized finance landscape.

However, yield farming isn't the only option to explore. Alpha Homora supports ETH loans and allows participants to become special users called liquidators and bounty hunters. We'll see what they mean later on in this chapter. The essential point is that all of these options allow users to earn based on their personal preferences and their risk appetite. Such features provide high APY returns, making Alpha Homora attractive to DeFi enthusiasts.

Alpha Homora's options for yield farming

The first option to explore in Alpha Homora is yield farming. Once their wallet is connected, the user can deposit funds, set up leverage and start farming immediately.

At the moment, the pools supported by Alpha Homora include the following.

- WETH / WBTC (Uniswap)
- WETH / USDT (Uniswap)
- WETH / USDC (Uniswap)
- WETH / DAI (Uniswap)
- WETH / DPI (IndexCoop)

A crucial aspect of yield farming via Alpha Homora is that every ALPHA token that is farmed is reinvested every day. According to the team, this offers higher profit potential in a completely passive way.

The ALPHA token explained

ALPHA is both a utility token and a governance token. It plays this role not only for the Alpha Homora protocol, but for other products in the Alpha Finance ecosystem as well. The ALPHA token is also the first project launched on both Binance Launchpad and Launchpool.

Use cases include providing liquidity, staking to receive a share of the protocol fees, and unlocking interoperability features between Alpha products.

In terms of governance, there are two aspects to consider. First of all, ALPHA token holders can manage key parameters of specific products, including interest rates, value ratios, liquidation penalties, and so on. The second point concerns the broader governance at the protocol level. According to Alpha Finance Lab, in the future ALPHA holders will be able to determine how the different Alpha products can work together more seamlessly.

The advantages of Alpha Homora

Innovation

Alpha Homora introduces new ways to participate in yield farming. These are useful for both yield farmers and the DeFi sector in general. Alpha Homora allows users to earn higher APYs without having to trust any intermediary.

Security audit

Smart contract audits are a key issue for investors. Several DeFi projects were launched without a proper security audit. Instead, Alpha Homora's smart contracts have been vetted and verified by Peckshield. Peckshield is a trust resource in the audit space.

Governance token

The addition of Alpha Homora to the Alpha Finance ecosystem introduces an additional synergy for the ALPHA token. As with other Alpha products, tokens are used in the governance of the Alpha Homora protocol. Involving the community is an important step towards long-term sustainability.

The risks of Alpha Homora

Liquidation

Be very careful with any strategy that includes leverage. You should only deposit funds if you fully understand the liquidation risks. At Alpha Homora, yield farmers run the risk of being liquidated. As long as users remain above 80% creditworthiness for Uniswap and 60% for IndexCoop, the positions will not be liquidated. This means that a leveraged position can be liquidated on Uniswap when the debt is more than 80% of the position value. This does not take slippage into account, so you need to be even more careful.

Potential vulnerabilities

Remember, code auditing does not mean that using the smart contract is safe. Bugs and vulnerabilities will always be part of any software. You need to keep this in mind when interacting with any smart contract.

Ethereum vault

By using Alpha Homora, you can earn interest on your Ether through an interest-bearing position. You can deposit ETH in Alpha Homora Bank and receive ibETH tokens in exchange. These ibETH tokens are tradable assets that accumulate interest and represent your share of ETH in the Bank's pool.

The interest paid by the ETH borrower is distributed to the ETH lender, in proportion to their share of the pool. The interest rate is determined by the Bank's utilization rate. The higher this rate is, the higher the interest rate will be. Simply put, the higher the demand for loans, the higher the interest rate.

A portion of the interest paid is sent to a treasury that acts as an insurance fund to offer protection from black swan events.

Liquidators and bounty hunters

Alpha Homora's platform offers other unique features. Special users called liquidators can liquidate risky positions. This happens when a user's position value falls below the settlement ratio for the respective platform. Hence, positions below the liquidation threshold run the risk of being liquidated manually. The liquidator receives 5% of the liquidated value as a commission.

Bounty hunters are another type of special user. They can use a function in the smart contract that sells all tokens obtained through yield farming in Alpha Homora's portfolio, converting them to Ether. By doing so, the bounty hunters reinvest the ETH collected in the yield farming pool, receiving 3% of the total reward. This, in turn, reduces the amount of ibETH tokens earned by the lender, as their share in the pool decreases.

The launch of Alpha Homora is an important milestone for the Alpha Finance ecosystem. The ability to open leveraged positions on liquidity mining is a significant innovation for the DeFi industry in general.

While yield farming is the main selling point, its interest-bearing Ethereum accounts can be attractive to more experienced users. Combined with the ability to become a liquidator or bounty hunter, the blockchain community has many ways to interact with this platform.

We have invested in ALPHA back in December 2020 and we have no plan in selling our coins. However, we have never tried the protocol ourselves.

Chapter 3 - Liquidity Pools

Liquidity pools are one of the core technologies behind the current DeFi ecosystem. They are an essential part of automated market makers, lending protocols, yield farming, synthetic assets, on-chain insurance, and blockchain video games.

In itself, the idea is really simple. A liquidity pool basically consists of funds put together in a large digital basket. But what can you do with these funds in a permissionless context, where anyone can add liquidity to it? Let's explore how DeFi leveraged the idea of liquidity pools.

What is a liquidity pool?

A liquidity pool is a collection of funds locked into a smart contract. Liquidity pools are used to facilitate decentralized trading and lending, as well as many other functions that we will explain later.

Liquidity pools are the backbone of many decentralized exchanges, such as Uniswap. Users called liquidity providers add an equal value of two tokens in a pool to create a market. In exchange for the funds provided, they receive the trading fees of the transactions carried out in the pool, in proportion to their share of the total liquidity.

Since anyone can become a liquidity provider, AMMs have made market making more accessible.

One of the first protocols to use liquidity pools was Bancor, but the concept gained more attention with the release of Uniswap. Other popular exchanges that use Ethereum liquidity pools are SushiSwap, Curve, and Balancer. The liquidity pools on these platforms contain ERC-20 tokens. Similar equivalents on Binance Smart Chain include PancakeSwap, BakerySwap, and BurgerSwap, whose pools contain BEP-20 tokens.

Liquidity pool vs. order book

To understand what sets liquidity pools apart, let's take a look at the fundamental component of trading: the order book. Simply put, the order book is a collection of the orders currently open for a given market.

The system that matches orders to each other is called the matching engine. Together with the matching engine, the order book is the foundation of any centralized exchange. This model is great for facilitating efficient trading and has enabled the creation of complex financial markets.

Trading in DeFi, on the other hand, involves executing on-chain trades, without a centralized party holding the funds. This presents a problem when it comes to order books. Each interaction with the order book requires gas fees, making it much more expensive to trade.

In addition to this, it also makes the work of market makers extremely expensive. Most importantly, most blockchains don't have the throughput capabilities needed to handle billions of dollars in exchanges every day.

This means that, on a blockchain like Ethereum, an on-chain exchange with the order book model is practically impossible. You can use side chains or layer-two solutions. However, the network in its current form cannot handle this throughput.

Before continuing, it should be noted that there are DEXs that work without problems with on-chain order books. Binance DEX is built on Binance Chain, and is designed specifically for fast and cheap trading. Another example is Project Serum, developed on the Solana blockchain.

However, since most of the assets in the crypto sector are located on Ethereum, it is not possible to trade them on other networks, unless you use some type of cross-chain bridge.

How do liquidity pools work?

Automated Market Makers are a significant innovation that makes on-chain trading possible without the need for an order book. Since no direct counterparty is needed to execute trades, traders can open and close positions on token pairs that would likely be highly illiquid on order book exchanges.

You can think of an order book exchange as a peer-to-peer system, where buyers and sellers are connected by the order book. For example, trading on Binance DEX is peer-to-peer as the operations take place directly between users' wallets.
Trading through an AMM is different. You can think of AMM trading as peer-to-contract.

As we have mentioned, a liquidity pool is a set of funds deposited into a smart contract by liquidity providers. When you trade on an AMM, you don't have a counterparty in the traditional sense of the term. Instead, you run it against the liquidity contained in the pool. In order for the buyer to buy, there must not be a seller at that particular time, as long as there is sufficient liquidity in the pool.

When you buy the new fashion token on Uniswap, there is no seller on the other side in the traditional sense. In reality, your business is managed by an algorithm that determines what happens in the pool. Furthermore, prices are also defined by this algorithm based on the operations carried out in the pool.

Obviously, liquidity has to come from somewhere, and anyone can become a liquidity provider. Therefore, this group could be seen in some sense as your counterpart. However, it differs from the order book model in that you are interacting with the smart contract that manages the pool.

The use of liquidity pools

So far, we have mainly talked about AMM, being the most popular application for liquidity pools. However, as we have already mentioned, cash aggregation is a profoundly simple concept, so it can be used in a lot of different ways.

One of these is yield farming or liquidity mining. Liquidity pools are the foundation of automated yield farming platforms such as yearn, where users add funds to pools which are then used to generate returns.

Distributing new tokens in the hands of the right people is a very difficult problem for crypto projects. Liquidity mining has been one of the most successful approaches. In practice, tokens are algorithmically distributed to users who deposit their tokens in a liquidity pool. After that, the newly issued tokens are distributed in proportion to each user's share in the pool.

Remember, these can also be tokens from other liquidity pools called token pools. For example, if you provide liquidity to Uniswap or lend funds on Compound, you will receive tokens representing your share of the pool. You may have the opportunity to deposit these tokens into another pool and make a profit. These chains can get quite complicated as protocols integrate token pools from other projects into their products.

We can also point to governance as a use case. In some projects, the threshold of token votes needed to submit a formal governance proposal is very high. If the funds are pooled, the participants can support a common cause they feel is important to the protocol.

Another emerging segment in DeFi is smart contract risk insurance. Many implementations of these services use liquidity pools.

Another, even more advanced, use of liquidity pools is tranching. It is a concept borrowed from traditional finance. It involves splitting financial products based on their risks and returns. Basically, these products allow LPs to select customized risk-return profiles.

The issuance of synthetic assets on the blockchain is also based on liquidity pools. Add collateral to a cash pool, link it to a trusted oracle, and you have a synthetic token anchored to any asset. In reality, it is a more complicated procedure, but the basic concept is simple.

The risks of liquidity pools

If you provide liquidity to an AMM, you need to pay attention to a concept called impermanent loss. In short, it is a dollar loss compared to the simple holding strategy when you provide liquidity to an AMM.

If you are providing liquidity to an AMM, you are likely exposed to impermanent loss. Sometimes it can be minimal, in other cases it can be huge.

Another danger to keep in mind are the risks of smart contracts. When you deposit funds into a cash pool, they are in the pool. Therefore, even if technically there are no intermediaries in possession of your funds, the smart contract itself can be considered a custodian. In the event of a bug or flash loan exploit, you could lose your funds forever.

Also, beware of projects whose developers have the ability to change the rules of the pool. Sometimes, developers may have an admin key or other type of privileged access in the smart contract code. This can allow them to potentially do something harmful, like take control of the funds in the pool.

Liquidity pools are one of the core technologies behind DeFi's current technology. They enable decentralization of trading, lending, generating returns and more. These smart contracts enable nearly every component of DeFi, and in all likelihood they will continue to do so for the foreseeable future.

Liquidity pools can be quite complicated and we do not recommend them to beginners.

Chapter 4 - Flash Loans

In previous chapters we have often mentioned flash loans, but we have never really explained what they are. In the next few pages we are going to do just that.

However, before we can talk about cryptocurrency flash loans we need to address how standard loans work.

Unsecured loans

An unsecured loan is a loan in which you do not have to provide any collateral. In other words, there isn't an asset that will go to your lender if you don't repay the loan. For example, suppose you really want a $3,000 gold necklace. You don't have the money you need, but you will have it when you get paid next week.

Therefore, you talk to your friend Bob and you explain to him how much you care about this necklace. Bob agrees to lend you the money. Provided, of course, that you pay it back as soon as you receive your salary.

Bob is a close friend of yours, so he didn't ask for a commission when he loaned you the $3,000. Not everyone will be so nice. Bob trusts you and is convinced that you will pay him back.

Another person may not know you, so they don't know if you could run away with their money.

Typically, unsecured loans from institutions require some type of credit check. They will analyze your track record to assess your ability to repay the debt. If they see that you have taken out several loans and paid them back on time, they may think you are quite reliable and lend you some money.

At that point, the institution transfers the money to you, with constraints. These constraints are interest rates. To get the money now, you have to accept that you will pay back a higher amount later.

You may already know this model if you use a credit card. If you don't pay a card for a certain period, you are charged interest until you repay your entire balance.

Secured loans

Sometimes a good credit score isn't enough. Even if you have repaid all of your loans on time for decades, you will have a hard time getting large-amount loans based solely on your creditworthiness. In these cases, you will need to provide collateral.

If you ask someone for a large loan, granting it is risky. To reduce the risk, the lender will force you to stake something. Your asset will go to the lender if you fail to repay the loan on time. The idea is that the lender can recover some of the value they have lost. Simply put, this is the collateral.

Suppose you want to buy a $50,000 car. Bob trusts you, but he doesn't want to give you money on an unsecured loan. Instead, he asks you to provide collateral. This could be your jewelry collection. Now, if you don't pay back the loan, Bob can take over your collection and sell it to recoup some of the money he lost.

Flash loans

We can include flash loans in the unsecured category simply because you don't provide any collateral. However, you don't have to go through a credit check or other similar procedure either. You just have to ask the lender if you can borrow $50,000 in ETH and you will be good to go.

Where's the catch? A flash loan must be repaid in the same transaction. This feature is not intuitive, but only because we are used to the format of a normal transaction where the funds move from one user to another. Like when you pay for goods or services, or deposit tokens on an exchange.

However, if you know about Ethereum, you will know that the platform is quite flexible. In the case of a flash loan, you can think of your transaction "schedule" as having three parts: get the loan, do something with the loan, repay the loan. And it all happens in a flash.

We can attribute this to the magic of blockchain technology. The transaction is transmitted to the network, temporarily lending you the funds. In the second part of the transaction, you can perform several actions. Do what you want, as long as the funds return in time for the third part. If not, the network rejects the transaction, so the funds go back to the lender. In reality, as far as the blockchain knows, the lender has always had the funds. This explains why the lender does not ask you for collateral. The contract to repay it is applied by the code.

What's the point of flash loans?

At this point, you are probably wondering why you should use a flash loan. If all of this happens in a single transaction, you can't buy a Lamborghini, right?

Well, that's not exactly the goal. Let's focus on the second part of the transaction described above, where you do something with the loan. The idea is to send the funds to a smart contract (or a series of smart contracts), generate a profit and return the initial loan when the transaction is complete. As you can see, the point of flash loans is to make money.

There are a couple of use cases where this might come in handy. Evidently, you can't do off-chain stuff in this time frame, but you can leverage DeFi protocols to make more money using your loan. The most popular applications of flash loans are in arbitrage, where you take advantage of the price disparities between different trading platforms.

Suppose a token is priced at $10 on DEX A, while on DEX B it costs $10.50. Assuming there are no commissions, buying ten tokens on DEX A and reselling them on DEX B would yield a profit of $5. This type of business won't allow you to buy a private island any time soon, but you can see how it allows you to make money by moving large volumes. If you buy 10,000 tokens for $100,000 and manage to resell them for $105,000, you will have a profit of $5,000.

If you get a flash loan, you can take advantage of arbitrage opportunities like this on decentralized exchanges. Here's an example of what the process might look like:

- Get a $ 10,000 loan
- Use the loan to buy tokens on DEX A
- Resell tokens on DEX B
- Repay the loan and any interest
- Enjoy your earnings

The beauty is that all of this happens in one transaction! However, realistically speaking, transaction fees, coupled with stiff competition, interest rates and slippage, make the margins for arbitrage very slim. You should find a way around the price differences to make the process profitable. When you compete against thousands of other users trying to do the same thing, you won't have much luck.

Flash loan attack

Cryptocurrencies and DeFi are a highly experimental sector. When so much money is at stake, it is only a matter of time before vulnerabilities are discovered. On Ethereum, we saw a striking example of this with The DAO hack in 2017. Since then, several protocols have suffered 51% attacks for financial gains.
In 2020, two high-profile flash loan attacks saw criminals steal nearly $1,000,000 in value at the time. Both attacks followed a similar pattern. Let's take a look at how they happened.

The first flash loan attack

In the first case, the borrower obtained an Ether flash loan on dYdX, a dApp dedicated to loans. The borrower split this loan and sent it to two other lending platforms: Compound and Fulcrum.

On Fulcrum, the borrower used a portion of the loan to short ETH against wrapped Bitcoin (WBTC). Therefore, Fulcrum had to buy WBTC. This information was passed on to another DeFi protocol, Kyber, which filled the order on Uniswap, a popular Ethereum-based DEX. However, due to Uniswap's low liquidity, the price of WBTC increased significantly, so Fulcrum overpaid for the WBTCs it bought.

At the same time, the borrower secured a WBTC loan on Compound using the remainder of the dYdX loan. When the price went up, the borrower moved the WBTCs on loan to Uniswap and made a modest profit. Finally, they repaid the loan on dYdX and pocketed the remaining ETH.

It sounds like a lot of work, and it might even be too hard to follow. The point is, the borrower used five different DeFi protocols to manipulate the markets. Incredibly, this all happened within the time frame that the original flash loan was confirmed.

The problem lies in the bZx protocol used by Fulcrum. By manipulating the market, the borrower managed to trick it into believing that WBTC was worth much more than it actually was. A pretty clever idea if you ask us.

The second flash loan attack

That was not a good week for bZx. A few days later, the protocol was hit by another attack. The borrower obtained a flash loan and converted part of it into a stablecoin called sUSD.

However, despite their name smart contracts are not very smart. They don't know how much stablecoins should cost. So when the manager placed a huge order to buy sUSD using the borrowed ETH, the price doubled on Kyber.

bZx believed that sUSD was worth $2 instead of $1. Afterward, the borrower took out a much larger loan of ETH than would normally have been possible on bZx, as their $1 coin had the purchasing power of $2. Finally, the manager repaid the initial flash loan and pocketed the rest.

Are flash loans risky?

Right or wrong, this particular attack model is impressive, because it demonstrates how far the bad guys can go. It is easy to look back at the methods used and say that bZx should have used a different price oracle to obtain data. The reality is that this type of theft is incredibly cheap: it doesn't require a particular investment on the part of the attacker. There was no financial deterrent that could stop them from succeeding.

Traditionally, individuals or groups who want to manipulate the market need huge amounts of cryptocurrency. With flash loans, on the other hand, anyone can become a whale for a few seconds. As we have seen, a few seconds is enough to pocket hundreds of thousands of dollars in Ether.

Looking on the bright side, the rest of the industry will learn from the two attacks. Is it possible that someone else will be able to carry out such an attack now that everyone knows about them? Maybe. Oracles have a number of weaknesses, as seen in the second attack, and they need considerable work to get rid of those vulnerabilities.

All in all, this does not depend on the flash loans and this form of DeFi lending could have many interesting use cases in the future, especially considering the low risks to creditors and debtors.

We have never taken a flash loan and we do not recommend them to you. Please, do not try to cheat this system, as hackers never end up well.

Chapter 5 - Atomic Swap

Atomic swaps consist of a technique that allows a quick exchange between two different cryptocurrencies, operating on distinct blockchain networks. This process is based on smart contracts, and allows users to buy and sell coins directly from their personal crypto wallet. In other words, atomic swaps are peer to peer exchanges across different blockchains.

Despite being an innovative technique, the idea of cross-chain trading has been the subject of discussion for many years. Tier Nolan was probably the first to describe a complete atomic swap protocol in 2013. However, in 2012 Daniel Larimer presented a trustless trading protocol called P2PTradeX which many consider to be the prototype of an atomic swap.

In the following years, several developers began experimenting with atomic swap protocols. The available data suggests that the Bitcoin, Litecoin, Komodo and Decred communities have played an important role in this process.

Apparently, the first peer to peer atomic swaps took place in 2014. But it wasn't until 2017 that the technique became known to the general public. This was mainly due to the successful swaps between LTC / BTC and DCR / LTC.

How do atomic swaps work?

Atomic swap protocols are designed to prevent deception by any participant. To understand how they work, let's assume Alice wants to exchange her Litecoin for Bob's Bitcoin.

First of all, Alice deposits her LTCs at the address of a contract that acts as a safe. Upon creating this safe, Alice also generates a key to access it. She then shares a cryptographic hash of the key with Bob. Bob can't access the LTCs yet because he only owns the hash of the key and not the key itself.

After that, Bob uses the hash provided by Alice to create another contract address, where he deposits his BTC. To claim the BTC, Alice must use the same key and, in doing so, she reveals it to Bob. This happens thanks to a special function called hashlock. This means that as soon as Alice claims the BTC, Bob is able to claim the LTC and the swap is closed.

The term 'atomic' refers to the fact that these transactions take place either entirely or not at all. If one of the participants gives up or doesn't do what they are supposed to do, the contract is canceled, and the funds are automatically returned to their owners.

Atomic swaps can take place in two different ways: on-chain and off-chain. On-chain atomic swaps take place on the network of one of the coins. In the example we just made, on the Bitcoin or Litecoin blockchain. Off-chain atomic swaps, on the other hand, take place on a secondary level. This type of atomic swap typically relies on two-way payment channels, similar to those used in the Lightning Network.

Technically speaking, most of these trustless trading systems are based on smart contracts that use multi-signature and Hash Timelock Contracts.

Hash Timelock Contracts (HTLC)

In addition to being an important part of Bitcoin's Lightning Network, Hash Timelock Contracts (HTLC) are also a key component that makes atomic swaps possible. As the name suggests, they rely on two central functions. A hashlock and a timelock.

A hashlock is what prevents the spending of funds unless a specific data is revealed. A timelock is a function that ensures that the contract can only be executed within a predefined interval. Consequently, the use of HTLC removes the need for trust as it creates a specific set of rules that prevents partial execution of atomic swaps.

Advantages of atomic swaps

The main advantages of atomic swaps are related to their decentralized nature. By removing the need for a centralized exchange or any other type of broker, cross-chain swaps can be performed by two parties without having to trust each other. They also provide an increased level of security as users don't have to trust their funds to a centralized exchange or third party. Instead, exchanges can take place directly from users' personal wallets.

Furthermore, this form of peer to peer trading has much lower operating costs as trading fees are either very low or absent. Finally, atomic swaps make it possible to execute exchanges very quickly, with higher levels of interoperability. In other words, it is possible to trade altcoins directly without using Bitcoin or Ethereum as an intermediary currency.

Limits

There are some conditions that must be met for the execution of an atomic swap, and could present obstacles to the widespread adoption of the technique. For example, to perform an atomic swap, the two cryptocurrencies must be based on blockchains that share the same hashing algorithm. In addition to this, they must be compatible with HTLC and other programmable features.

Atomic swaps raise user privacy concerns. This is because on-chain exchanges and transactions can be tracked on a blockchain explorer. This allows the easy linking of addresses. A short-term solution to this problem is the use of privacy-focused cryptocurrencies to reduce exposure. However, many developers are experimenting with the use of digital signatures in atomic swaps as a more reliable solution.

The importance of atomic swaps

Atomic swaps have great potential to improve the cryptocurrency industry and have yet to be tested on a larger scale. Cross-chain trading can solve many of the problems that affect most centralized exchanges. Some of these problems include the following.

- Greater vulnerability. Keeping many valuable assets in one place alone makes them vulnerable to cyberattacks. Therefore, centralized exchanges are prime targets for digital theft.

- Poor management of funds and human error. Centralized exchanges are operated by people. If those in important roles make mistakes or if leaders make poor choices regarding the operation of the exchange, users' funds can be compromised forever.

- Higher operating costs. Centralized exchanges have higher trading and withdrawal fees.

- Inefficiency in terms of volume demand. When market activity becomes too intense, centralized exchanges often fail to handle the increased demand. This causes the system to slow down or disconnect.

- Legislation. In most countries, cryptocurrency legislation is far from ideal. There are still many problems surrounding government approval and management.

Although atomic swaps are still quite new and have limitations, this technology is bringing significant changes in interoperability between blockchains and in the possibilities of cross-chain trading. As such, the technology has great potential to influence the growth of the cryptocurrency industry, opening new avenues for decentralization and peer to peer money transfers. It is very likely that atomic swaps will be used more and more in the future, especially within decentralized exchanges.

Chapter 6 - NFTs

The creation of Bitcoin introduced the concept of trustless, digital rarity. Before its launch, the cost of replicating something in the digital world was almost nil. With the advent of blockchain technology, programmable digital rarity has become possible and is now used to map the digital world to the real world.

Non-fungible tokens (NFTs), also often referred to as crypto collectibles, further develop this idea. Unlike cryptocurrencies, where all tokens are created equally, non-fungible tokens are unique and limited in quantity.

NFTs are one of the building blocks of a new blockchain-based digital economy. Several projects are experimenting with NFTs for a variety of use cases, including video games, digital identity, licensing, certificates, and artwork. Additionally, they can also allow for fractional ownership of high-value items.

As NFTs are becoming easier to issue, new types of assets are created every day. This chapter will explain what NFTs are, what they can be used for, and how a game called CryptoKitties congested the Ethereum blockchain in late 2017.

What are NFTs?

A non-fungible token is a type of cryptographic token on a blockchain that represents a single asset. It can be an entirely digital asset or tokenized versions of assets in the real world. Since NFTs are not interchangeable with each other, they could function as a proof of authenticity and ownership in the digital world.

Fungibility means that the individual units of an asset are interchangeable and essentially indistinguishable from each other. For example, fiat currencies are fungible, as each unit is interchangeable with any other equivalent individual unit. A ten dollar bill is interchangeable with any other genuine ten dollar bill. This is imperative for an asset that aims to serve as a medium of exchange.

Fungibility is a desirable property for a currency, as it allows for free trade and, theoretically, there is no way to know the history of each individual unit. However, this is not a useful feature for collectibles.

What if instead we could create digital assets similar to Bitcoin, with the difference of a unique identifier for each unit? This would make each of them different from all other units. This is an NFT.

How NFTs work

There are various frameworks for creating and issuing NFTs. The best known of these is ERC-721, a standard for issuing and trading non-fungible assets on the Ethereum blockchain.

A newer and improved standard is the ERC-1155. It allows a single contract to contain both fungible and non-fungible tokens, opening up a whole new range of possibilities. The standardization of NFT issuance enables a higher degree of interoperability, which ultimately benefits users. Basically it means that unique assets can be transferred between different applications with relative ease.

If you want to keep and contemplate your awesome NFTs, you can do it with Trust Wallet. Just like other blockchain tokens, your NFT exists on one address. It is important to note that NFTs cannot be replicated or transferred without the owner's permission. Not even the issuer of the NFT can do that.

NFTs can be traded in open markets, such as OpenSea. These markets connect buyers with sellers, and the value of each token is unique. Of course, NFTs are subject to price changes in response to market supply and demand.

But how can these things have any value? Just like any other precious object, the value is not inherent in the object itself but is assigned by people who believe it to be precious. In essence, value is a shared belief. It doesn't matter whether it's fiat money, precious metals or a vehicle. All these things have value because people believe they have it. This is how every precious object (including NFTs) acquires value.

The use of NFTs

NFTs can be used by decentralized applications to issue unique digital items and crypto collections. These tokens can be a collectible, an investment product, or something else.

The economics of video games are nothing new. Furthermore, considering that many online games already have their own economy, using blockchain to tokenize gaming assets is a simple step forward. In fact, the use of NFT could potentially solve or mitigate the inflation problem common to many video games.

While virtual worlds are already thriving, another interesting use of NFTs is the tokenization of assets in the real world. These NFTs can represent fractions of physical assets that can be stored and exchanged as tokens on a blockchain. This could introduce new and necessary liquidity into different markets, such as works of art, real estate, and rare collectibles.

Digital Identity is also an industry that can benefit from NFT properties. Storing identification and ownership data on the blockchain would increase privacy and data integrity for many people around the world. At the same time, easy and trustless transfers of these assets could reduce friction in the global economy.

The history of CryptoKitties and Ethereum

One of the first NFT projects that gained significant traction was CryptoKitties, a game developed on Ethereum that allows players to collect, breed and trade virtual cats.

Each CryptoKitty can have a combination of various different properties, such as age, race or color. Therefore, each of them is unique, and they cannot be interchanged with each other. Furthermore, they are indivisible, meaning there is no way to divide a CryptoKitty token into multiple parts.

CryptoKitties gained notoriety after congesting the Ethereum blockchain due to the intense activity that rocked the network. As of April 2021, the all-time high for the number of daily transactions on the Ethereum blockchain is still around the height of the popularity of CryptoKitties. It is clear that the game has caused a great impact on the Ethereum network, but other factors have also contributed to this record, including the popularity of Initial Coin Offerings.

While a controversial topic, CryptoKitties is a fun prime example of a blockchain use case that isn't a coin, but something used for recreational and leisure purposes. Collectively, these virtual cats have moved millions of dollars, and some of the rarest units have sold for hundreds of thousands of dollars.

Famous projects using NFT and crypto collectibles

Many projects already use NFTs as collectibles and trade items. Here is a selection of some of the best known.

Decentraland

Decentraland is a decentralized virtual reality world where players can own and trade pieces of virtual land and other in-game NFT items. Cryptovoxels is a similar game where players can build, develop and trade virtual property.

Gods Unchained

Gods Unchained is a digital trading card game where cards are issued as NFTs on the Ethereum blockchain. Since each digital card is unique, players can own and trade them for the same level of ownership as physical cards.

My Crypto Heroes

My Crypto Heroes is a multiplayer role-playing game in which players can level up historical heroes through missions and battles. Heroes and in-game items are issued as tokens on the Ethereum blockchain.

Binance Collectibles

Binance Collectibles are NFTs issued in partnership between Binance and Enjin for special occasions. If you want to collect them, be sure to follow Binance on Twitter and stay tuned for the next giveaways. If you want to participate in an NFT giveaway, follow these steps:

- Download a wallet that supports Ethereum, such as MetaMask.
- Copy your Ethereum address and provide it according to the giveaway rules. You may have to submit it through a form or leave it in a Twitter comment. Be sure to double-check the rules to find out what to do in order to participate.
- If you have won an NFT and it has been distributed, you will see it in the Collectibles tab of MetaMaks. From here, you can sell it in a P2P marketplace like OpenSea.

Crypto Stamps

Crypto Stamps are issued by the Austrian Postal Service and connect the digital world with the real one. These stamps are used to carry mail like any other stamp, but are also saved as digital images on the Ethereum blockchain, making them a digitally exchangeable collector's item.

Digital collectibles open blockchain technology to entirely new possibilities, outside of conventional financial applications. By representing physical assets in the digital world, NFTs have the potential to become a crucial part of the economy in general.

The use cases are numerous, and it is likely that many developers will introduce new and exciting innovations for this promising technology.

We absolutely love NFTs and we hold some Crypto Punks and Hashmasks.

Chapter 7 - Elastic Offer Tokens

Decentralized Finance has seen an explosion of new types of financial products on the blockchain. We have already talked about yield farming, Bitcoin tokenized on Ethereum, Uniswap and flash loans. Another interesting emerging segment of the crypto sector includes tokens with elastic offers, or rebase tokens.

The particular mechanism on which they are based allows a lot of experimentation. Let's see how these tokens work.

What is an Elastic Offer Token?

A token with an elastic offer works by expanding or reducing the supply in circulation based on changes in its price. The increase or decrease occurs through a mechanism called rebase. With rebase, the token supply is algorithmically increased or decreased, based on the current price of each token.

In some ways, elastic bidding tokens can be compared to stablecoins. They try to keep a target price, and these rebase mechanisms facilitate the process. However, the key difference is that rebase tokens do so with a mutable offer.

Wait, aren't there a lot of cryptocurrencies already operating with a changing offering? In a certain way, yes. Currently, 6.25 new BTCs are issued with each block. After the 2024 halving, this sum will be reduced to 3.125 per block. It's a predictable rate, so we can estimate how many BTCs will exist next year or after the next halving.

Elastic bidding tokens work differently. As mentioned, the rebase mechanism adjusts the token's offer periodically. Let's say we have an elastic offering token that aims to hold a value of 1 USD. If the price is above 1 USD, the rebase expands the current offer, reducing the value of each token. Conversely, if the price is below 1 USD, the rebase reduces the offer, increasing the value of the token.

What does this mean from a practical point of view? The amount of tokens in users' wallets changes when a rebase occurs. Suppose you own Rebase USD (rUSD), a hypothetical token that tries to hold a price of 1 USD. We have 100 rUSD safe in our hardware wallet. Let's assume the price falls below USD 1. After running the rebase, we will only have 96 rUSD in our wallet, but at the same time, each coin will be worth more than before the rebase.

The idea is that the proportion of your funds to the total offer has not changed with the rebase. If you had 1% of the offer before the rebase, you should still have 1% after the event, even if the number of coins in your wallet has changed. Essentially, you hold your share of the network regardless of the token price. It is a pretty fascinating subject, because rebase tokens have a lot of potential. Let's take a look at a couple of examples.

Ampleforth

Ampleforth is one of the first coins created with an elastic offering. Ampleforth proposes itself as an unsecured synthetic commodity, where 1 AMPL has a target price of 1 USD. Rebase events happen every 24 hours.

The project was relatively unknown before the introduction of a liquidity mining campaign called Geyser, which was particularly interesting for its duration. The scheme distributes tokens to participants over a 10-year period. Geyser is a great example of how liquidity incentives can create significant interest in a DeFi project.

While technically a stablecoin, AMPL's price chart shows how volatile bidding tokens can be.

It may make more sense to represent tokens with elastic supply in terms of market capitalization. Since the price of individual units is less important, the market cap can be a more accurate parameter of the growth and spread of the network.

Yam Finance

Yam Finance is another elastic offering token that is gaining some popularity. The overall design of the Yam protocol is something of a combination of Ampleforth's elastic offering, Synthetix's staking system, and the fair launch of yearn.finance. YAM is also aiming for a target price of USD 1.

YAM is a community experiment, as all tokens were distributed via liquidity mining. There was no premine, no allocation to founders. In other words, the playing field for acquiring these tokens was the same for everyone through a yield farming program.

As a completely new and unknown project, Yam reached $600 million in locked-in value in its staking pools in less than two days. What may have attracted a lot of liquidity is the fact that YAM's farming was aimed specifically at the most popular DeFi tokens: COMP, LEND, LINK, MKR, SNX, ETH, YFI, and Uniswap's ETH-AMPL LP tokens.

However, due to a bug in the rebase mechanism, a lot more offer than expected has been issued. Afterwards, the project was launched again and migrated to a new smart contract thanks to a joint effort and a community-funded audit. Now the future of Yam is completely in the hands of the owners of YAM.

The risks of Elastic Offer Tokens

Elastic offer tokens are highly risky and very dangerous investments. You should only invest if you fully understand what you are doing. Remember, looking at the price charts won't be very helpful, as the amount of tokens you own will change after rebases.

Sure, this can amplify the gains on the upside, but it can also multiply the losses. If the rebase event happens while the token price is falling, you will not only lose money from the price drop, but you will also own fewer tokens after each rebase!

Being quite difficult to understand, investing in rebase tokens will likely result in a loss for most traders. Invest only in tokens with elastic offers that you understand well. Otherwise, you will not be in control of your investment and will not be able to make informed decisions.

Elastic bidding tokens are one of the must-follow innovations in DeFi. As we have seen, they are coins and tokens that can algorithmically adjust their offer to try to maintain a target price.

Are Elastic Bidding Tokens just an interesting experiment, or will they gain significant popularity? It's hard to say, but there are new DeFi protocol designs under development that seek to further advance this idea.

We have not invested in Elastic Offer Tokens and we do not plan to do it any time soon. The volatility of cryptocurrency is already pretty high, there is no need to add a complicated rebase system to the mix.

Chapter 8 - The Coin Burn Process

In previous chapters we have mentioned this process. It is time to dive deeper into what it is and how it influences the economy of cryptocurrencies that do it.

The coin burning process aims to permanently remove coins from the market, reducing the total supply. To explain how this works and why, we will use BNB as an example.

Binance carries out periodic Coin Burn events through the use of a smart contract function known as a burn function. BNB coin burning events are scheduled for each quarter until 100,000,000 BNB tokens are destroyed, which is 50% of the total BNB issued (200,000,000 BNB).

The number of BNB coins to be destroyed is based on the number of operations performed on the exchange over a period of 3 months. Then, at the end of each quarter, Binance destroys BNB based on the overall trading volume.

The burn process

Basically, a token burn event occurs in the following order.

First of all, a holder of the coin invokes the burn function, declaring that they want to 'burn' a certain amount of coins. The token contract verifies that this person actually has the coins in their wallet, as well as checking that they have not declared an invalid number, such as 0 or -5. Only positive numbers are allowed. If the person does not have enough coins, or if the declared number is invalid, the burn will not be performed. If they have enough coins, the coins will be subtracted from the wallet. After that, the total supply of the coin will be updated, and the coins will be eliminated. By performing the burn function, the declared coins are destroyed and become inaccessible.

Some scammy projects, like Safemoon, offer coin burn events to incentivize people to buy their tokens, given the deflationary nature. However, normally scam coins have a gigantic supply in the first place, so coin burns in those cases are just a marketing tactic.

Chapter 9 - MetaMask

During the entirety of this book, we have mentioned MetaMask quite a few times. However, if you are just starting out with cryptocurrency, you might find it difficult to set it up for yourself. Therefore, we have decided to dedicate this chapter to a deep explanation of this useful wallet.

Ethereum brought with it the promise of a distributed internet, the long-awaited Web 3.0. An equal playing field characterized by the absence of central points of failure, effective data ownership and decentralized applications.

The infrastructure is gradually taking shape with an industry-wide focus on decentralized finance and interoperability protocols that aim to connect the various blockchains. It is now possible to trade tokens and cryptocurrencies with trustless methods, take out crypto-backed loans, and even use Bitcoin on Ethereum.

For many Ethereum enthusiasts, MetaMask is the go-to wallet. Unlike normal smartphone or desktop software, it comes as a browser extension, which allows users to interact directly with the web pages that support it. In this chapter, we will explain how MetaMask works and walk you through the first steps of using it.

What MetaMask is

MetaMask is an open source Ethereum wallet that supports all kinds of Ethereum-based tokens (such as those using the ERC-20 standard, or non-fungible tokens). Furthermore, you can receive them from others, or buy and trade them with the integrated services of Coinbase and ShapeShift.

What makes MetaMask very interesting is its ability to interface with websites. Using other wallets you should copy and paste payment addresses or scan a QR code on a separate device. With the MetaMask extension, the website simply connects to your wallet, and asks you to accept or decline the transaction.

MetaMask can function like a normal crypto wallet, but its real strength is the smooth interaction with smart contracts and decentralized applications. Let's see how to set it up.

Install MetaMask

The MetaMask wallet can be installed on Google Chrome, Firefox or Brave browsers. It is also available on iOS and Android, but we won't talk about it in detail. In this chapter we will refer to Firefox, but the steps will be more or less identical on each platform chosen.

First of all, you need to visit the official download page on metamask.io. Here you need to select your browser and you will be redirected to the Chrome web store or Firefox add-on site. Click on the button to add the extension to your browser. You may need to grant some permissions before it is up and running. Make sure you don't have a problem with the level of access it has on your browser.

Initializing the wallet

You should now see a welcome message, just click on "Get Started". You will be asked to import a seed phrase or create a new one. Click on Create a Wallet. The next page asks if you want to send anonymized data to help developers improve the app. Select the option you prefer.

Now you need to create a password. If you are one of those legendary creatures who really read the terms of use of the software they use, you can find them by clicking on Terms of Use. Otherwise, think of a strong password, tick the box and click Create.

The seedphrase backup

This step is so important that it deserves a chapter of its own. MetaMask is a non-custodial service, so no one else can access your funds, not even the MetaMask developers. Your tokens exist in a sort of encrypted vault inside your browser, protected by your password. This means that if your computer is lost, stolen or destroyed, no one can help you recover the wallet. Your private keys will be lost forever in cyberspace.

Therefore, it is vital to write down the backup phrase. It is the only way to recover your account if something unfortunate happens. We recommend that you write down the words and store them in two or three different locations. You don't have to bury them in a fire-resistant vault in the heart of the forest, but it sure doesn't hurt.

Funding the wallet

In this chapter, we will refer to the Ropsten testnet. It is a network that works almost exactly like the real Ethereum network, but its units are worthless. These fake tokens come in handy when you're developing smart contracts and want to make sure they don't have vulnerabilities that allow hackers to steal $50 million worth of crypto with two clicks. Every step we perform on this network will be replicable on the real Ethereum network.

To access the Ropsten testnet, click on Main Ethereum Network in the upper right corner and select Ropsten Test Network.

We will use a faucet to receive fake funds to play with.

You can click on the little fox icon at any time to see a pop-up with your MetaMask account information. Move your mouse to

Account 1 and click to copy your Ethereum address. Paste it into the form and click on Send me test Ether.

Ethereum transactions are generally confirmed rather quickly, but it may take some time for 1 ETH to arrive in your wallet. Check if you have received it by clicking on the fox in your toolbar.

Once there, you can start interacting with the dApps.

Unlocking the decentralized web

Since we are on a testnet, we don't have such a large choice of applications to use. For a full list of decentralized applications on the mainnet, check out State of the DApps or Dappradar. You can play video games, buy unique assets, or bet on prediction markets.

MetaMask and privacy

It is important to be careful what you are authorizing. If a website knows your address, it can see all Ether and Token transactions involving your it. Also, it can link it to your IP address.

Some prefer to separate their addresses to avoid overlaps, while others don't care about these risks. The level of privacy you want to achieve is fundamentally up to you. As a general rule, don't grant access to websites you don't trust.

Exchange Ether for DAI

Time to do our first swap. In this example we will convert to DAI, an ERC-20 token that acts as a stablecoin. Like our Ether testnet, this DAI has no real value. Click on Select a token, add the Uniswap Default List, and select DAI. Alternatively, you can also choose WETH (wrapped ether).

It remains only to enter the amount of ETH we want to exchange. By doing this, we will see an estimate of how many DAI we are about to receive.

MetaMask will ask for your intervention again. In this case, you will need to confirm the transaction before it is created. Make sure the fees are okay when doing this on the mainnet, they can be substantial.

After that, we just have to wait for the transaction to be confirmed.

Where are your tokens?

Your Ether has disappeared, but your account is not showing the tokens. Don't worry, you just have to add them manually.

For the most popular tokens, you can select Add Token in your wallet and search for the name or ticker. For those less known (or those on the testnet), you need to add the contract address. This is an identifier that tells MetaMask where to look for our balance.

MetaMask offers other useful features that we haven't mentioned yet. You can also connect a hardware wallet, create a contact list and, of course, receive and send funds as you would with a normal wallet. Take a look at the settings to customize the extension according to your needs.

Aside from that, the usual security principles apply: MetaMask is a hot wallet, so it runs on an internet-connected device. This exposes you to greater risk than a cold wallet, which is kept offline to reduce the risk of potential attacks.

The MetaMask app

The MetaMask app for Android / iPhone offers a viable solution for interacting with Web3 apps on the go. With many of the same features found on the extension, it integrates a dApp browser to access various decentralized applications at the touch of a button.

The application procedures are very similar to those of the browser extension. You can make direct transfers of Ether or tokens from your wallet, or even interact with Uniswap as we have seen above. MetaMask is a powerful tool for navigating the decentralized web. Currently, there are more than one milion people using MetaMask every single day.

As the Ethereum network develops, applications like MetaMask will undoubtedly become integral components in the bridge between existing technologies and the new cryptocurrency infrastructure.

Chapter 10 - Other Wallets

In the previous chapter we have talked about MetaMask. However, there are different types of wallet you can use to store your crypto. Let's take a look at the different solutions you have.

How cryptocurrency wallets work

Contrary to popular belief, crypto wallets do not actually contain cryptocurrencies. Instead, they provide the tools needed to interact with a blockchain. In other words, these wallets can generate the information needed to send and receive cryptocurrencies via blockchain transactions. Among other things, this information contains one or more public and private key pairs.

The wallet also contains a public address, i.e. an alphanumeric identifier generated based on public and private keys. An address of this type is a specific "location" on the blockchain to which coins can be sent. This means that you can share your public address with other people to receive funds, but you don't have to disclose your private key to anyone.

The private key allows you to access your cryptocurrencies, regardless of which wallet you use. So even if your computer or smartphone is compromised, you can still access your funds from another device, as long as you have the corresponding private key. Remember that coins never really leave the blockchain, they are only transferred from one address to another.

Hot wallet vs. cold wallet

As already mentioned, cryptocurrency wallets can be "hot" or "cold," depending on how they operate.

A hot wallet is any wallet connected in some way to the Internet. For example, when you create an account on MetaMask and send funds to your wallet, you are depositing into a hot wallet. These wallets are quite simple to create, and the funds are quickly accessible, making them practical for traders and for those who use crypto frequently.

Cold wallets, on the other hand, are not connected to the Internet. Instead, they use a physical means to store keys offline, which makes them resistant to online cyber attack attempts. As a result, cold wallets tend to be a much safer alternative to storing your coins. This method is also known as cold storage and is particularly suitable for long-term investors.

Software wallet

Software wallets come in different varieties, each with unique characteristics. Most are connected to the Internet in some way. Below you will find brief descriptions of some of the most common and important types of software wallets.

Web Wallet

You can use a web wallet to access the blockchain via a browser interface without having to download or install anything. This includes both exchange wallets and other browser-based wallet providers.

In most cases, you can create a new wallet and set a personal password to access it. However, some providers keep and manage private keys on your behalf. While this may be more convenient for inexperienced users, it is a dangerous practice. If you don't have your own private keys, you are entrusting your money to someone else. To address this problem, many web wallets allow you to manage your keys. Therefore, it is important to check the technical approach of each wallet before choosing the most suitable one for you.

When using cryptocurrency exchanges, you should consider using the available protection tools.

Desktop Wallet

As the name suggests, a desktop wallet is software that you download and run locally on your computer. Unlike some web-based versions, desktop wallets offer full control over your keys and funds. When you generate a new desktop wallet, a file called "wallet.dat" is stored on your computer. This file contains the private key information used to access your addresses, so you should encrypt it with a personal password.

If you encrypt your desktop wallet, you will be prompted to provide the password each time you run the program to authorize the wallet.dat file. If you lose this file or forget your password, you will most likely have lost access to your funds.

Consequently, it is vital that you backup your wallet.dat file and keep it in a safe place. Alternatively, you can export the corresponding private key or seed phrase. By doing this, you will be able to access your funds from other devices, in case your computer stops working or becomes inaccessible in some way.

In general, desktop wallets can be considered more secure than most web versions, but it is important to check that your computer is free from viruses and malware before creating and using a cryptocurrency wallet.

Mobile Wallet

Mobile wallets work similarly to their desktop counterparts but are specifically designed as smartphone applications. This type of wallet is quite practical as it allows you to send and receive cryptocurrencies through the use of QR codes.

As a result, mobile wallets are particularly suitable for daily transactions and payments, making them a viable option for spending Bitcoin, BNB and other cryptocurrencies in the real world. MetaMask is a great example of a cryptocurrency mobile wallet.

However, like computers, mobile devices are vulnerable to malicious apps and malware attacks. Therefore, it is recommended to encrypt your mobile wallet with a password, as well as back up your private keys to protect your funds in case of loss or breakage of your smartphone.

Hardware Wallet

Hardware wallets are electronic devices that use Random Number Generation to create public and private keys. The keys are then stored on the device itself, which is not connected to the Internet. Therefore, hardware-type wallets are cold wallets and are considered one of the safest options.

Although these wallets offer much higher levels of security against online attacks, they could present risks if the firmware implementation is not performed correctly. Additionally, hardware wallets tend to be less user-friendly, and it is more difficult to access funds than it can be with a hot wallet.

You should consider using a hardware wallet if you intend to hold your crypto for a long time or if you have large amounts of cryptocurrencies. Currently, most hardware wallets allow you to set a PIN code to protect the device, as well as a recovery phrase.

Paper Wallet

A paper wallet is a piece of paper on which a public address and its private key are physically printed in the form of QR codes. Scanning these codes allows you to perform cryptocurrency transactions.

Some paper wallet websites offer the ability to download the code to generate new addresses and keys offline. Therefore, these wallets are highly resistant to online cyber attacks and can be considered as an alternative to cold storage.

However, due to the numerous weaknesses the use of paper wallets is currently considered dangerous and not recommended to beginners. If you want to use a paper wallet, it is essential to understand the risks associated with it. An important weakness of paper wallets is that they do not allow you to send partial funds, but only the entire balance sheet in one go.

For example, imagine you generate a paper wallet to which you have sent several transactions, for a total of 10 BTC. If you decide to spend 2 BTC, you should first send all 10 coins to another type of wallet (e.g., a desktop wallet), and spend 2 BTC from there. You can then send the 8 BTC back to a new paper wallet, although a hardware or software wallet would be a better choice.

Technically speaking, by importing the private key of your paper wallet into a desktop wallet and spending only part of the funds, the remaining coins would be sent to a "different address" which is automatically generated by the Bitcoin protocol. If you do not manually set the new address as the address you control, it is likely that you will lose your funds.

Most of today's software wallets handle this on your behalf, sending the remaining coins to an address that is part of your wallet. However, it is important to remember that your paper wallet will be empty after its first outgoing transaction.

The importance of backups

Losing access to your cryptocurrency wallets can be very costly. Therefore, it is important to make backups regularly. In many cases, backing up wallet-dat files or seed phrases is sufficient. Essentially, seed phrases play a very similar role to private keys but are generally easier to manage. If you have decided to add a password, remember to include it in the backup as well.

Chapter 11 - Multisig Wallets

There is a special type of wallet that is used by advanced cryptocurrency enthusiasts, because it offers major improvement regarding security. We are talking about multisig wallets and this chapter is going to dive deeper into this topic.

Multisig means multi-signature, a term that describes a specific type of digital signature that allows two or more users to sign documents as a group. As a result, a multi-signature is produced through the combination of several unique signatures. Multisig technology is widespread in the world of cryptocurrencies, but the principle has existed long before the creation of Bitcoin.

In the context of cryptocurrencies, the technology was first applied to cryptocurrency addresses in 2012, eventually leading to the creation of multisig wallets a year later. Multisig addresses can be used in a variety of contexts, but most cases have to do with security issues.

The way they work

To use a simple analogy, we can imagine a safe with two locks and two keys. Alice owns the first key and Bob owns the second key. The only way to open the box is to provide both keys at the same time, so one of the owners cannot open the box without the other's consent.

In practice, it is possible to access funds within a multi-signature address only by using 2 or more signatures. Consequently, the use of a multisig wallet allows users to create an additional level of security for their money. Before continuing, it is important to understand the basics of a standard Bitcoin address, which is based on a single key.

Single-key vs Multisig

Generally speaking, bitcoins are stored in a standard single-key address, so anyone with the corresponding private key is able to access the funds. This means that you only need a key to sign the transactions and that those who have the private key can transfer the coins whenever they want, without the need for authorization from others.

Even though managing a single-key address is faster and easier than a multisig one, it presents a number of problems, especially when it comes to security. By having only one key, the funds are protected by a single point of vulnerability. For this reason, hackers continue to develop new phishing techniques to try to steal the funds of cryptocurrency users.

Furthermore, single-key addresses are not the most suitable option for companies dealing with cryptocurrencies. Suppose that the funds of a large company are stored within a standard address, with a single corresponding private key. This would imply that the private key would be given to a single person or several people at the same time. This is a method which is clearly not very secure.

Multisig wallets offer a potential solution to both problems. Unlike single-keys, funds stored in a multisig address can only be moved when multiple signatures are provided.

Depending on how the multisig address is configured, it may require a different combination of keys. The most common is 2-of-3, where 2 are sufficient to access the funds of a 3-signature address. However, many other variations exist, such as 2-of-2, 3-of-3, and 3-of-4.

There are several possible applications for this technology. Here are some of the most common use cases of multi-signature wallets for cryptocurrencies.

Increase security

By using a multisig wallet, users are able to prevent problems caused by the loss or theft of a private key. Therefore, even if one of the keys is compromised, the funds remain safe.

Suppose Alice creates a 2-of-3 multisig address and she keeps each private key in a different place or device (e.g., cell phone, laptop, and tablet). Even if her cell phone was stolen, the thief would not be able to access her funds using only 1 of the 3 keys. The same is true for phishing attacks and malware, which are less likely to succeed as hackers would be able to access a single device and a single key.

In addition to cyber attacks, if Alice loses one of her private keys, she can still access her funds using the other 2 keys.

Two-factor authentication

By creating a multisig wallet that requires two keys, Alice is able to establish a two-factor authentication mechanism to access her funds. For example, she might keep a private key on her laptop, and one on her cell phone. By doing so, she would have the guarantee that only someone with access to both keys can carry out a transaction.

However, keep in mind that using multisig technology for two-factor authentication can be dangerous. This is true in the case of a 2-of-2 multisig address. If one of the keys is lost, it will not be possible to access the funds. Therefore, using a 2-of-3 setup or a third-party 2FA service that offers backup codes would be safer. In the case of accounts on exchange platforms, the use of Google Authenticator is strongly recommended.

Escrow transactions

Creating a 2-of-3 multisig wallet allows for an escrow transaction between two parties, Alice and Bob, that includes a third party, Charlie, as a trusted judge in case something goes wrong.

In such a scenario, Alice would deposit the funds, which would be blocked. Thereafter, if Bob provides the goods or services as agreed, the two parties can use their own keys to sign and complete the transaction.

Charlie, the judge, should only intervene in the event of a dispute. At this point Charlie could use a key to create a signature to give the funds to Alice or Bob, based on her decision.

Decision process

A board of directors could use a multisig wallet to control access to company funds. For example, by setting up a 4-of-6 wallet and giving each one a key, no board member would be able to misuse the funds. Consequently, only decisions that have been agreed by the majority could be enforced.

Disadvantages

While multisig wallets are a viable solution to a number of problems, it is important to remember the associated risks and limitations. Setting up a multisig address requires some technical knowledge, especially if you don't want to rely on third party vendors.

Furthermore, given that blockchain and multisig addresses are both relatively new, it may be difficult to seek legal help if something goes wrong. There is no legal custodian of funds deposited in a wallet shared with several people in possession of a key.

Despite some disadvantages, multisig wallets have numerous interesting applications, making Bitcoin and other cryptocurrencies even more useful and attractive. This is especially true for businesses. By requiring more than one signature to transfer funds, multisig wallets provide greater security and allow for trustless escrow transactions. Therefore, it is very likely that this technology will be used more and more in the future.

We have used multisig wallets in the past, when we needed to put an escrow in place. They have worked well for us and we recommend them for those special occasions.

Chapter 12 - Initial Coin Offering (ICO)

We have mentioned the term ICO a few times during the course of this book. In this chapter we are going to dive deeper into this topic. Let's get right into it.

An Initial Coin Offering is a fundraising method through the use of cryptocurrencies. It is mainly used for projects that have not yet fully developed their blockchain platform, product or service. Payment is typically made with Bitcoin or Ethereum, but fiat currencies are also accepted in some cases.

Investors participate in the Initial Coin Offerings with the hope that the company will succeed. In fact, this would result in increasing demand and cause an increase in value in the underlying token. In other words, they hope to get a good return on investment as early supporters of this particular project.

How ICOs work

ICOs are often compared to IPOs (Initial Public Offering). However, this comparison is rather misleading. Typically, IPOs are used by established businesses that sell partial ownership shares to raise funds. Instead, ICOs are mainly used as a fundraising mechanism that allows businesses to raise capital for their project in its early stages. Furthermore, investors who buy tokens are not acquiring any ownership in the company.

Typically, tokens distributed in ICOs are created on the Ethereum blockchain, according to the ERC-20 token standard. This means they are ERC-20 tokens. In addition to Ethereum, there are other platforms that support the creation and issuance of digital tokens (e.g. Stellar, NEM, NEO and Waves). Conversely, companies that already have a functioning blockchain often choose to issue digital assets on their platform. Taking ERC-20 tokens as an example, a company could use Ethereum smart contracts to create and issue their own digital token. The ERC-20 protocol defines a set of rules that the company must follow in order to issue a token on the Ethereum blockchain, and the smart contract ensures that these rules are followed in a trustless way.

Once the founders of the start-up have created their token, they have to convince investors to participate in the ICO. In order to do this, a whitepaper is created that describes the company's goals and how the new ecosystem should operate. The founders could pair this document with a website that offers more information about the people involved in the ICO and why they believe in the success of the project.

The purpose of ICOs

An ICO can be a very effective method of raising venture capital and financing. For start-ups, it allows you to receive funds based on an idea, which may or may not have been tested on the market. Many of these small, unconsolidated businesses would likely fail to raise funds any other way. Traditional financial institutions would not lend capital on the basis of a whitepaper alone. This is especially in the crypto sector, where the lack of regulation has caused reluctance on the part of these institutions.

While new businesses and start-ups make up the majority of ICOs, things are changing. Some established companies are starting to recognize the value of ICOs and the decentralization potential offered by cryptocurrencies. Some of these have organized ICOs to launch new projects on a blockchain-based system in order to raise capital or decentralize their business. This practice is called "reverse ICO."

Can Anyone Do an ICO?

The short answer is yes. With the right guidance, almost anyone could develop a token and write a whitepaper describing its eventual application. However, the company or individuals who do this must create a viable blockchain project. This requires knowledge, skills and experience that not everyone has. It is also necessary to adhere to the complex network of laws and regulations that vary from one jurisdiction to another and which may soon be modified in response to the growing popularity of ICOs.

To organize a successful ICO, the company should be solid and supported by concrete evidence of how the project or idea will work, why it is valid, what it consists of, who needs it and how it can be developed. Selling the idea and convincing investors to buy is a critical phase towards positive results.

The regulation of ICOs

The growing number of ICOs has attracted the attention of regulatory authorities around the world. Nowadays, crypto regulation is a hot topic in the community. Within the US, the SEC and the CFTC are two regulatory institutions that are discussing the regulatory framework for ICOs and cryptocurrencies.

The regulation of the ICO sector is still in its early stages, and there is no uniformity between different countries. On the one hand, too much regulation risks hindering the growth and development of this emerging sector. On the other hand, there are those who argue that regulation would bring greater legitimacy to the space, alleviating the fears of traditional financial institutions that have so far been reluctant towards it. A balanced approach is preferred by those who believe that the crypto ecosystem should not be a financial "wild west", but at the same time it should have enough freedom to operate outside the limits of the traditional financial system.

While some countries, such as China and South Korea, have outlawed all ICOs, the U.S. SEC has issued a detailed statement on the subject, recommending potential investors to apply due diligence before committing to new investments. The SEC also disclosed that some ICOs may qualify as securities, and as such are subject to relevant federal regulations.

The importance of ICOs

ICOs use cryptocurrencies as their primary funding tool and, as such, offer a new avenue for individuals and innovative businesses who want to act differently. The crypto ecosystem is attracting more and more attention thanks to the large capital raised by blockchain start-ups. Despite this, the ICO method could lead to both favorable and unfavorable results. While scams and large public failures negatively impact cryptocurrency reputation, successful activities bring the industry greater authenticity in the public eye.

ICO tokens that see reliability and widespread adoption could eliminate some of the uncertainties that alienate institutions and consumers from the cryptocurrency industry. Although this new investment method has problems to solve, it is considered by many to be a valid alternative to traditional fundraising practices and could become a compelling approach for several companies in the future.

We have invested in some ICOs and they have always been a wild ride. We do not recommend them to beginners or those that have small capitals. Do not play the "angel investor" game in the world of cryptocurrency, it never ends well.

Chapter 13 - Initial Exchange Offering (IEO)

In the previous chapter we have discussed the complicated world of ICOs. However, ICOs are not the only way crypto companies have to raise funds. Another popular practice is IEOs and in this chapter we are going to tell you more about them.

Often an IEO is made when a new crypto project wants to launch its cryptocurrency or blockchain product but requires significant capital to do so.

The IEO model differs from the Initial Coin Offering in that it is made possible with the help of a cryptocurrency exchange, such as Binance or Coinbase. Projects can raise funds by engaging the exchange's customer base and launch trading for their token a little later.

There are several thousand cryptocurrencies and blockchain projects in existence or under development. Most projects require some kind of financial incentive to keep developers and contributors involved. Not all projects can count on donations or contributions from generous investors. More often than not, funding is needed during the development phase.

There are many different ways for developers to raise capital. Trying to obtain finance from venture capital investors can be time-consuming. Issuing a project's coins before its launch and keeping them in a treasury is another option, but it often receives criticism from the community.

Choosing to organize an IEO can be an interesting possibility, assuming the developer has an action plan and is willing to develop the vision of the project.

What an IEO is

As the name suggests, an Initial Exchange Offering (IEO) involves using a cryptocurrency exchange to raise funds for a new project. Asset trading is common on these platforms, but it generally only happens after developers have raised funds to start their own projects.

With an IEO, potential investors can buy these assets before they are available on the market. With the help of the exchange that facilitates the sale of tokens, registered users who have provided KYC information will be able to buy tokens before trading on the free market begins.

Since the IEO is facilitated by an exchange, startups that choose this option will need to be serious about their action plan. In most cases, the IEO proposal is subject to strict scrutiny by the exchange involved. In a way, exchanges put their reputation on the line for every IEO they decide to offer.

Organizing an IEO

Even though blockchain technology is relatively new, there are thousands of startups and crypto companies in the industry. Many of these are competing to acquire potential investors via ICO or IEO events.

When the developers of a crypto project decide to organize an IEO, they have to go through a complicated procedure before they can raise the first dollar.

Several requirements must be met for the project team. Having a solid business model, experienced members, a good use case for the technology, and a detailed white paper are absolutely crucial factors. Organizing an IEO is similar to declaring a long-term commitment to the success of the project.

Additionally, they must determine whether the Initial Exchange Offering will have a hard cap or a soft cap. A hard cap guarantees a limit on the amount of money that can be invested. A soft cap sets an initial goal to reach but allows the developers to raise more money later on.

Once these decisions have been made, it is time to choose an exchange platform to carry out the IEO. Binance Launchpad has helped dozens of projects raise the necessary investment capital. Some examples include BitTorrent, Band Protocol , Axie Infinity, Alpha Finance Lab, and WazirX. Other exchanges have launched their own platforms for IEOs, each with their own benefits, requirements and potential drawbacks.

Why blockchain projects choose IEO

Raising funds for a new crypto or blockchain project can be quite difficult. Similar to any other industry, there is a lot of competition to attract investors. Not everyone can successfully attract investment capital with traditional methods.

An IEO can be useful as it targets existing cryptocurrency holders. As the participating exchange helps lend credibility to the fundraising project, there is a certain degree of trust. After all, the exchange is risking its reputation by facilitating the IEO. However, all interested parties should carry out extensive research before making any financial commitment.

For projects looking to raise money with the help of an exchange, an IEO is a reliable option. Most Initial Exchange Offerings reach their funding goal very quickly, depending on the vision and use cases involved. Furthermore, the project token will be listed on the exchange at the end of the sale.

IEO vs. ICO

On paper, the concept of the IEO could be similar to that of the ICO. During the ICO bubble on Ethereum in 2017-2018, ICOs were organized practically every day. Many projects raised millions of dollars, but there were also a lot of deceptive offers, as well as outright scams. With no one openly "examining" ICOs, the concept eventually evolved into the IEO, which many consider more reliable. Many ICOs have broken US security laws, resulting in various lawsuits and refunds to investors.

Participating in an ICO entailed significant risks. Investors had to send Bitcoin or Ether to a smart contract or website and hope to receive their tokens. Anyone with basic smart contract knowledge and web development skills could create a shiny website with a promising roadmap and start raising money. It was far from ideal and carried a huge risk to anyone investing in ICOs.

IEOs largely mitigate these risks. Investors send money through exchange wallets, instead of sending it directly to the project. Dishonest projects or teams with poor business skills will not be able to conduct a successful IEO, due to very stringent requirements.

Furthermore, an IEO has lower risks and more flexibility than ICOs. The listing of the token on the exchange organizing the sale is guaranteed. For investors, this allows them to close the position whenever they want.

The risks and opportunities of an IEO

While each IEO is reviewed by the exchange, no investment is risk-free. It is possible that the fundraising project will not be able to realize its vision. This can affect the price of the token, regardless of its value during the IEO.

That said, IEOs can also present favorable investment opportunities. Having the ability to buy tokens in advance knowing that they will be listed on markets with good liquidity can create good opportunities. However, not all IEO tokens will increase in value once trading begins.

The lower frequency of IEOs has helped eliminate some of the less recommendable projects in the crypto and blockchain industry. Even if no method is foolproof, it appears that IEOs are at least on the right track.

Just because the IEO exists doesn't mean everyone should invest in these offerings. It is always recommended to do your own due diligence, regardless of how companies and projects raise capital. Contributing funds to an IEO offers benefits, but the risks cannot be ignored.

We like to participate in IEOs only when they are held on an exchange we trust. Stay away from shady exchanges that pretend to offer the next 100x coin. The exchange should be impartial and not advertise the IEO too aggressively.

Chapter 14 - Decentralized Exchanges (DEXs)

Initial exchange offerings can be done on decentralized exchanges as well. In this chapter we explain what they are and how they work.

Since the early days of Bitcoin, exchanges have played a vital role in matching cryptocurrency buyers and sellers. Without these forums that welcome a global user base, we would end up with much less liquidity and no way to agree on the correct price of assets.

Traditionally, centralized operators have dominated this field. However, with the rapid evolution of available technologies, more and more tools for decentralized exchanges continue to emerge.

Definition of decentralized exchanges

In theory, any peer-to-peer exchange could constitute a decentralized exchange. In this chapter we are mainly interested in a platform that emulates the functions of centralized exchanges. The key difference is that its backend exists on a blockchain. Nobody takes custody of your funds, and you don't have to trust the exchange to the same extent as centralized alternatives.

How a centralized exchange works

With the typical centralized exchange, you deposit your funds. When you deposit a cryptocurrency, you give up its control. Not from a usability point of view, as you can still use it for trading or withdraw it, but from a technical point of view: you can't spend it on the blockchain.

You don't have the private keys associated with the funds, so when you withdraw your coins, you need to ask the exchange to sign a transaction on your behalf. When trading, transactions don't take place on-chain. In fact, in this case the exchange only modifies users' balances in its database.

The overall procedure is incredibly optimized because the slowness of the blockchains does not hinder trading, and it all happens within the system of a single entity. It's easier to buy and sell cryptocurrencies, and you have more tools at your disposal.

This is possible by sacrificing independence. In fact, you have to entrust your money to the exchange. As a result, you expose yourself to some counterparty risk. What happens if the team runs away with your hard earned BTC? What if a hacker paralyzes the system and drains the funds?

For many users, this is an acceptable level of risk. They simply rely on reputable exchanges with excellent records and precautions to mitigate data breaches.

How a decentralized exchange works

DEXs are similar to their centralized counterparts in some respects, but noticeably different in others. First of all, there are different types of decentralized exchanges available to users. The common theme between them is that orders are executed on-chain and that users don't sacrifice custody of their funds at any point in the process.

Despite the considerable work done on cross-chain DEXs, the most popular platforms revolve around assets on a single blockchain.

Order book on-chain

In some decentralized exchanges, everything happens on-chain. Each order is recorded on the blockchain. This is probably the most transparent approach, as you don't have to trust a third party to pass orders and there's no way to obfuscate them.

Unfortunately, it is also the least practical. Since you are asking every node in the network to register the order forever, you end up paying a commission. You have to wait for a miner to add your message to the blockchain. Therefore, it could take a while to see your transaction go through.

Some identify front running as a flaw in this model. Front running occurs in markets when an insider is aware of a pending transaction and uses this information to place a trade before the transaction is processed. The front runner takes advantage of information unknown to the public. Generally speaking, this practice is illegal.

Obviously, if everything is published on a global ledger, there are no front running opportunities in the traditional sense. Instead, it is possible to launch a different type of attack, where a miner sees the order before it is confirmed, and has their order added to the blockchain first.

Examples of on-chain order book models include the Stellar and Bitshares DEXs.

Off-chain order book

DEXs with off-chain order books are still decentralized in some respects, but it must be recognized that they have a greater degree of centralization than the previous category. Instead of recording orders on the blockchain, they are stored on another server.

You may find a centralized entity with full control of the order book. If this entity is dishonest, it could deceive the markets to some extent (through front running or order forgery). However, you would still take advantage of the non-custodial solution.

The 0x protocol for ERC-20 tokens and other standards on the Ethereum blockchain is a good example of this type of DEX. Instead of acting as a single DEX, it provides a participant framework known as a relayer to manage off-chain order books. Using 0x smart contracts and other tools, it is possible to tap into a combined liquidity pool and transmit orders between users. The operation is performed on-chain only when the two counterparties are combined.

These approaches are better in terms of usability than on-chain order book structures. They don't face the same speed limits, as they don't use the blockchain to the same extent. However, the trade must be adjusted to it, so the off-chain order book model remains inferior to centralized exchanges in terms of speed.

Off-chain order book implementations include Binance DEX, IDEX, and EtherDelta.

Pros of DEXs

No KYC

Compliance with KYC / AML measures are the norm for many exchanges. For legislative reasons, individuals are often required to present identification and proof of residence.

This process is an accessibility problem for some users. What if you don't have valid documents available? What if the information is disclosed in some way? Since DEXs are permissionless, no one checks your identity. All you need is a cryptocurrency wallet.

However, there are certain legal requirements when DEXs are partially managed by a central authority. In some cases, if the order book is centralized, the group managing it must comply with the rules.

No counterparty risk

The main advantage of decentralized cryptocurrency exchanges is the fact that they do not own client funds. Therefore, even catastrophic incidents like the hack against Mt. Gox in 2014 could not endanger funds or reveal sensitive user information.

Unlisted tokens

Tokens not listed on centralized exchanges can still be traded freely on DEXs, as long as there is supply and demand.

Cons of DEX

Usability

Realistically, DEXs are far less user-friendly than traditional exchanges. Centralized platforms offer real-time operations unaffected by the timing of the blockchain. For beginners who are not familiar with non-custodial cryptocurrency wallets, CEXs offer a more forgiving experience. If you forget your password, you can simply reset it. However, if you lose your seed phrase, your funds are lost in cyberspace.

Trading volumes and liquidity

The trading volume on DEX is nothing compared to that on CEXs. Perhaps more importantly, CEXs tend to have higher liquidity as well. Liquidity is a measure of how easily you can buy or sell assets at a reasonable price. In a highly liquid market, bid and ask prices present little difference, indicating great competition between buyers and sellers. In an illiquid market, you will have a harder time finding someone willing to trade the asset for a reasonable price.

DEXs are still relatively new, so they don't always provide supply or demand for the crypto assets you want to trade. You may not be able to find the trading pair you want, and in any case the assets may not be priced appropriately.

Commissions

Commissions aren't always higher on DEXs. However, they can be, particularly when the network is congested or if you're using an on-chain order book.

Over the past few years, many decentralized exchanges have emerged, each developed on the basis of previous attempts to optimize the user experience and build more powerful trading platforms. Ultimately, the idea seems to align perfectly with the etho of self-determination: as with cryptocurrencies, users don't have to rely on a third party.

Conclusion

Congratulations on making it to the end of this book, we hope you found some useful insights to take your cryptocurrency trading skills to the next level. As you should know by now, the world of cryptocurrency is extremely complicated and there is a new "opportunity" every way you look. However, our experience tells us that only by taking things seriously and having a proper plan you can develop your investing skills to the point that you can actually accumulate wealth.

Our final advice is to stay away from the shining objects that the world of cryptocurrencies offers you every day. Simply study the world of cryptocurrencies in depth and when you feel ready try to invest a little bit of money. Analyze your results, improve your money management skills and become the master of your emotions.

As you can see, there are no shortcuts you can take. Easy money does not exist. What exists is the possibility to start from zero and work your way up to become a professional cryptocurrency investor. The journey might be difficult, but it is certainly worth it.